MEDITERRANEAN DIET COOKBOOK

150 EASY FLAVORFUL RECIPES FOR AN HEALTHIER LIFESTYLE. INCREASE YOUR PHYSICAL WELL-BEING AND KEEP YOUR BODY WEIGHT UNDER CONTROL

By Susan Lombardi

Introduction

The Mediterranean Diet is not just a diet but it's a way of life. This diet offers a really extended range of fresh and delicious foods from all food categories but even more. It's a different way to eat, to prepare and cook food. And we can say – no doubt - a healthier way.

The Mediterranean diet gives you the chance to enjoy many lovely dishes and even if there is more of a focus on certain food groups none are excluded.

Furthermore, this diet gives the opportunity to learn how to appreciate and prepare more fresh and seasonal food and change radically your habits. This change start including your family members. The more that are attempting this healthy lifestyle, the more likely there will be a positive outcome. Having a support system that you can depend on really comes in handy, especially when trying a radical lifestyle change.

Switch to a new diet making a lifestyle change can be tough! This book will help you step-by-step to afford this journey and will prepare you to understand this culinary tradition and all its shades and finally benefit from it lifelong.

In this book, I will be sharing with you all you need to know about the Mediterranean diet and how to get started.

Let's begin!

Chapter 1: What is the Mediterranean diet?

The Mediterranean diet is an eating pattern that follows the traditional method for eating in the nations surrounded by the Mediterranean Sea. You don't need to live in Italy, Spain or France to profit by the diet, be that as it may; numerous individuals are changing to it for the scope of health benefits it gives.

The Mediterranean diet is not a strict plan. Or maybe, it's a method for eating that emphasizes natural products, vegetables, whole grains, vegetables and olive oil. Fish is the principle protein source rather than red meat, pork or poultry. And indeed, it remembers red wine-for balance. Aged dairy are consumed normally but in moderate sums. Eggs and poultry are occasionally expended, but red meat and prepared foods are not eaten normally.

The Mediterranean diet is associated with lower cholesterol, decreased danger of coronary illness and stroke, lower danger of Parkinson's and Alzheimer's diseases and a more drawn out life. Developing exploration shows it might also lessen danger of, and advantage those with, sadness, tension, type 2 diabetes and a few cancer growths.

If you are searching for a healthy way to lose the weight and to maintain an optimal health, then this is the best diet for you. It's the Mediterranean diet, a very popular and unique one.

The Mediterranean diet refers to the traditional eating habits and lifestyles of people living around the Mediterranean Sea – Italy, Spain, France, Greece, and some North African countries. The Mediterranean diet has become very popular in recent times, as people from these regions have better health and suffer from fewer ailments, such as cancer and cardiovascular issues. Food plays a key role in this.

Research has uncovered the many benefits of this diet. According to the results of a 2013 study, many overweight and diabetic patients showed a surprising improvement in their cardiovascular health after eating the Mediterranean diet for 5 years. The study was conducted among 7000 people in Spain. There was a marked 30% reduction in cardiovascular disease in this high-risk group.

The report took the world by storm after the New England Journal of Medicine published the findings. Several studies have indicated its many health benefits – the Mediterranean diet may stabilize the level of blood sugar, prevent Alzheimer's disease, reduce the risk of heart disease and stroke, improve brain health, ease anxiety and depression, promote weight loss, and even lower the risk of certain types of cancer.

The diet differs from country to country, and even within the regions of these countries because of cultural, ethnic, agricultural, religious, and economic differences. So there is no one standard Mediterranean diet. However, there are several common factors.

The Mediterranean Diet Pyramid

The Med diet food pyramid is a nutrition guide to help people eat the right foods in the correct quantities and the prescribed frequency as per the traditional eating habits of people from the Mediterranean coast countries.

The pyramid was developed by the World Health Organization, Harvard School of Public Health, and the old ways Preservation Trust in 1993.

There are 6 food layers in the pyramid with physical activity at the base, which is an important element to maintain a healthy life.

Just above it is the first food layer, consisting of whole grains, breads, beans, pasta, and nuts. It is the strongest layer having foods that are recommended by the Mediterranean diet. Next comes fruits and vegetables. As you move up the pyramid, you will find foods that must be eaten less and less, with the topmost layer consisting of foods that should be avoided or restricted.

The Mediterranean diet food pyramid is easy to understand. It provides an easy way to follow the eating plan.

The Food Layers: *Whole Grains, Breads, Beans* – The lowest and the widest layer with foods that are strongly recommended. Your meals should be made of mostly these items. Eat whole-wheat bread, whole-wheat pita, whole-grain roll and bun, whole-grain cereal, whole-wheat pasta, and brown rice. 4 to 6 servings a day will give you plenty of nutrition.

Fruits, Vegetables – Almost as important as the lowest layer. Eat non-starchy vegetables daily like asparagus, broccoli, beets, tomatoes, carrots, cucumber, cabbage, cauliflower, turnips 4 to 8 servings daily. Take 2 to 4 servings of fruits every day. Choose seasonal fresh fruits.

Olive oil – Cook your meals preferably in extra-virgin olive oil. Daily consumption. Healthy for the body, it lowers the low-density lipoprotein cholesterol (LDL) and total cholesterol level. Up to 2 tablespoons of olive oil is allowed. The diet also allows canola oil.

Poultry, cheese, yogurt – The diet should include cheese, yogurt, eggs, chicken, and other poultry products, but in moderation. Maximum 2-3 times in a week. Low-fat dairy is best. Soy milk, cheese, or yogurt is better.

Meats, sweets – This is the topmost layer consisting of foods that are best avoided. Red meats you can have them once or twice in a weekly max, sweets only one time at month. Remember, the Mediterranean diet is plant-based. There is very little room for meat, especially red meat. If you cannot live without it, then take red meat in small portions. Choose lean cuts. Have sweets only to celebrate. For instance, you can have a couple of sweets after following the diet for a month.

Recommended Foods: For example, most people living in the region eat a diet rich in whole grains, vegetables, fruits, nuts, seeds, fish, fats, and legumes. It is not a restrictive diet like the many low-fat eating plans. Actually, fat is encouraged, but only from healthy sources, such as polyunsaturated fat (omega-3 fatty acids) that you will get from fish and monounsaturated fat from olive oil.

It is strongly plant-based, but not exclusively vegetarian. The diet recommends limiting the intake of saturated fats and trans fats that you get from red meat and processed foods. You must also limit the intake of dairy products.

Fruits and vegetables – Eat daily. Try to have 7-10 servings every day. Meals are strongly based on plant-based foods. Eat fresh fruits and vegetables. Pick from seasonal varieties.

Whole grains – Eat whole-grain cereal, bread, and pasta. All parts of whole grains – the germ, bran, and the endosperm provide healthy nutrients. These nutrients are lost when the grain is refined into white flour.

Healthy fats only – Avoid butter for cooking. Switch to olive oil. Dip your bread in flavored olive oil instead of applying margarine or butter on bread. Trans fats and saturated fats can cause heart disease.

Fish – Fish is encouraged. Eat fatty fish like herring, mackerel, albacore tuna, sardines, lake trout, and salmon. Fatty fish will give you plenty of healthy omega-3 fatty acids that reduce inflammations. Omega-3 fatty acids also reduced blood clotting, decreased triglycerides, and improves heart health. Eat fresh seafood two times a week. Avoid deep-fried fish. Choose grilled fish.

Legumes – Provides the body with minerals, protein, complex carbohydrates, polyunsaturated fatty acids, and fiber. Eat daily.

Dairy and poultry – You can eat eggs, milk products, and chicken throughout the week, but with moderation. Restrict cheese. Go for plain or low-fat Greek yogurt instead of cheese.

Nuts and seeds – 3 or more servings every week. Eat a variety of nuts, seeds, and beans. Walnuts and almonds are all allowed.

Red meat – The Mediterranean diet is not meat-based. You can still have red meat, but only once or twice a week max. If you love red meat, then make sure that it is lean. Take small portions only. Avoid processed meats like salami, sausage, and bologna.

Olive Oil – The key source of fat. Olive oil will give you monounsaturated fat that lowers the LDL or low-density lipoprotein cholesterol and total cholesterol level. Seeds and nuts will also provide you monounsaturated fat. You can also have canola oil but no cream, butter, mayonnaise, or margarine. Take up to 4 tablespoons of olive oil a day. For best results, only take extra-virgin olive oil.

Wine – Red wine is allowed, but with moderation. Don't take more than a glass of red wine daily. Best take only 3-4 days a week.

Desserts – Say no to ice cream, sweets, pies, and chocolate cake. It's better to replace sweets with fresh fruits.

Main Components: *Focus on natural foods* – Avoid processed foods as much as you can;

Be flexible – Plan to have a variety of foods;

Consume fruits, vegetables, healthy fats, and whole grains daily;

Have weekly plans for poultry, fish, eggs, and beans;

Take dairy products moderately;

Limit red meat intake;

Take water instead of soda. Only take wine when you are having a meal.

The Med Lifestyle

Not just the food, but the correct lifestyle is also equally important. This includes both getting adequate exercise and making social connections.

Physical Activity – It is at the base of the food pyramid, even lower than the first and most important food layer – getting adequate physical activity is essential. This includes exercising regularly, swimming, biking, running, and playing an active sport. However, there are other ways as well to maintain good health.

You will find many from the Mediterranean region not going to the gym. But, they are not inactive. Many are into a lot of manual labor. They will walk to their workplace, to the bakery, or the farmer's market. They walk to their friend's home. Even a daily walk and moderate exercise will help. Natural movements are good. Avoid the escalator. Take the stairs instead.

How much exercising is good? Working out is always good for health. You don't have to lift weights, though. 10-15 minutes on the treadmill and gym bike 5 days a week should be good. Half an hour of moderate-intensity activity will do. Nothing better if you can also do a few muscle-strengthening activities twice a week. You can also try walking 200 minutes a week or even gardening for an hour 4-5 times a week.

Cook at Home – Home cooked food is always healthier than eating out. For example, restaurant cooked pasta will have higher portions of sodium. Again, you can have one portion of whole-grain spaghetti with tomato sauce and spinach instead of the heavy cream sauce. You can control the ingredients by preparing the meals at home. Home cooked meals have lots of minerals, vitamins, and fiber, and are lower in added sugar, sodium, and saturated fat.

Eat Together – The mealtime should be a social experience. Eating together with friends or family is a great source of energy and helps reduce stress. It will boost your mood, which will have a positive impact on your physical health. Plus, it will prevent you from overeating too. You will often find the Mediterranean people eating together in a garden.

Switch the TV off and enjoy your meal. Monitor what the kids are eating. If you live alone, invite a co-worker, neighbor, or friend. You can even invite someone and prepare meals together.

Laugh Often – Have you heard of the popular saying, "Laughter is the best medicine"? This is true in the Mediterranean culture. Many are individuals with a big personality. Their conversations are full of humor. They love to tell stories. Enjoy life and keep a positive attitude.

Live a Simple Life – Consider food, for example. You won't find them buying too much of anything. The idea of buying any ingredient in bulk is foreign to them. They buy fresh, focusing on daily needs. And of course, fresh food is always best.

Enjoy Every Bite – Slow down and enjoy each bite. Many will eat for survival. But in the Mediterranean belt, they love their food. They enjoy it. Don't eat on the go. Sit down and have a proper meal.

Chapter 2: Benefits of the Mediterranean Diet

Heart disease and stroke – The Mediterranean diet recommends limited eating of processed foods, red meat, and refined breads, which contributes towards a lower risk of heart ailments and stroke. A study carried out over 12 years among 25,000 women found that women eating this diet were able to reduce their risk of heart disease by 25%.

The **PREDIMED** (study was carried out amongst men and women with a high-risk of cardiovascular disease and type-2 diabetes in Spain. After 5 years of research, it was discovered that those who had a calorie-unrestricted Mediterranean diet had a 30% lower risk of heart issues.

Alzheimer's – Research also suggests that the diet can improve blood sugar levels, cholesterol, and blood vessel health, which in turn may lower the risk of dementia and Alzheimer's disease. A 2018 study (scanned the brains of 70 people for dementia and monitored their food habits. After 2 years, it was observed that those on the Mediterranean diet had fewer protein plaques or beta-amyloid deposits than others, and thus a lower risk of Alzheimer's.

Other studies have also revealed that the Mediterranean diet may also prevent the decline of thinking skills and memory with age as there is an increased supply of oxygen and nutrients to the brain.

The diet is packed with antioxidants, such as olive oil and nuts, which may delay mental decline. A link between consuming fish and lower risk of Alzheimer's has also been found.

Diabetes – The diet with healthy carbs and whole grains offers big benefits like stabilizing the blood sugar level. Complex whole grain carbs like wheat berries, buckwheat, and quinoa improves overall energy and keeps the sugar level even in your blood. Research on more than 400 people between the age of 55 and 80 years have revealed that the Mediterranean diet can lower (the risk of type-2 diabetes by 52%. This study was carried out over 4 years.

Parkinson's disease – The diet is rich in antioxidants, which may prevent oxidative stress or cell damage, thus reducing the risk of Parkinson's disease by as much as 50%.

Weight loss – The Mediterranean diet gives you plenty of fiber that will make you feel satiated. You won't overeat as a result. The diet improves metabolism and promotes healthy weight loss. Just remember to focus on consuming fibrous vegetables, fruits, beans, and legumes instead of simple carbohydrates. This is a safe and sustainable way to lose weight as almost nothing is denied in the overall meal plan. The U.S. News & World Report ranked Mediterranean diet #1 in the 'Best Overall Diet' category for 2019.

Cancer – The diet has also been linked to a lower risk of certain types of cancer. Researchers looked at the findings of 83 studies covering more than 2 million people and concluded that it may reduce (the risk of breast, gastric, colorectal, and colon cancer. The cancer mortality rate is significantly lower amongst those who eat this diet. This has been attributed to the higher intake of whole grains, vegetables, and fruits. The result of this study was published in the Nutrients journal.

Another study according to the JAMA Internal Medicine journal discovered that women eating this diet were able to reduce the risk of breast cancer by 62%.

Inflammation – Fatty fish like tuna, mackerel, and salmon have a lot of omega-3 fatty acids that can reduce inflammation. Besides, the omega-3 will also improve the elasticity of your skin and make it stronger.

Rheumatoid arthritis – In this autoimmune disease, the body's immune system attacks the joints by mistake, causing swelling and pain. The National Institutes of Health's Office of Dietary Supplements has suggested that long-chain omega-3 fatty acids, which you will find in fatty fish provides relief from the symptoms of RA or Rheumatoid arthritis.

Good for the gut – The Med diet provides 7% more good bacteria in the microbiome, compared to those eating a traditional western diet as it is a plant-based eating plan with a lot of fruits, vegetables, nuts, seeds, and legumes. This improves gut health.

Several other scientific studies have also revealed the health gains of eating this diet.

The Rockefeller Foundation – This was one of the first studies on the diet carried out on the Greek island of Crete. The Greek government asked for help from the Rockefeller Foundation after the World War II because the island was severely destructed after the war and the people were in abject poverty. Many field staff were sent, including nutritionists and nurses.

They visited many homes and took notes on their food and drinking habits. To their surprise, it was found that most people were of good health and were living into old age in spite of the poverty. Very few people were suffering from heart disease, though 40% of their calories were coming from fat.

Ancel Keys' 7 Country Study – This was a follow-up study to find out the heart health condition of residents around the Mediterranean Sea. It was carried out in the late 1950s by Ancel Keys, the American scientist. In the late 1950s, 92 out of 1000 men in the United States were suffering from heart diseases. But in Crete, Ancel found to his surprise, that only 3 men out of 1000 had heart conditions.

The University of Barcelona Study – In recent time, the University of Barcelona Carried out a study on 7000 men and women over 5 years. They found that there were significant improvements in heart health when the participants ate a Mediterranean diet. The risk of cardiovascular disease dropped by almost 30%. And they were also high-risk individuals, as the participants were all overweight people, and also diabetics and smokers. The results of this 2013 study was published by the New England Journal of Medicine.

The Cochrane Study – Carried out in the same year, this study too arrived at the same conclusion. The researchers concluded by noting that a high-protein, high-fiber, low-glycemic index, low-carbohydrate diet improves cardiovascular health and reduces the risk of diabetes.

Hundreds of studies have been carried out in recent years to verify whether the diet improves health or not. Almost all of them have concluded that those who eat a Mediterranean diet have lower risks of Alzheimer's, dementia, and diabetes. Many other health advantages have also been noted.

Chapter 3: What Foods Can I Eat On This Diet?

The heft of your diet ought to incorporate regular, natural Mediterranean foods. This diet is extremely unrestrictive, and you'll have the option to appreciate a lot of delectable foods. You may even find some new top choices!

You should go for a wide assortment of foods, to guarantee that you're getting an equalization of supplements, nutrients, and minerals. Whole, single fixing foods are basic for benefiting as much as possible from your Mediterranean lifestyle.

Concentrate on eating:

Tubers: These dull vegetables ought to be expended with some restraint, but are as yet a significant piece of this diet. Appreciate potatoes, sweet potatoes, turnips, and yams.

Whole grains: Avoid refined sugars, but eat small servings of things like whole oats, darker rice, rye, grain, corn, buckwheat, whole wheat, and whole grains.

Poultry: Occasionally, appreciate chicken, duck, turkey, or different winged animals.

Healthy fats: This is a significant piece of the Mediterranean diet, so ensure you're getting a lot of fats from olive oil, nuts, and avocado.

Also, you ought to make certain to drink a lot of water, as well as a moderate measure of red wine, espresso, and tea. Note that anybody with issues with alcohol use ought to abstain from consuming wine, despite the fact that it is energized with this diet.

Avoid These Unhealthy Foods

You ought to maintain a strategic distance from these unhealthy foods and ingredients:

Added sugar: Soda, candies, frozen yogurt, table sugar and numerous others.

Tran's fats: Found in margarine and different handled foods.

Processed meat: Processed hotdogs, franks, and so on.

Highly handled foods: Anything marked "low-fat" or "diet" or which seems as though it was made in a manufacturing plant.

You should peruse food names cautiously if you want to dodge these unhealthy ingredients.

What to Drink

Water ought to be your go-to drink on a Mediterranean diet.

This diet also incorporates moderate measures of *red wine* — around 1 glass for every day. Nonetheless, this is totally discretionary, and wine ought to be maintained a strategic distance from by anybody with liquor abuse or issues controlling their use.

Espresso and tea are also totally adequate, but you ought to keep away from sugar-improved refreshments and natural product juices, which are exceptionally high in sugar.

Chapter 4: How to follow the Mediterranean diet. Tips and tricks

Plan your meals – Plan your meals in advance. Plan what you want to eat throughout the week when you have time during the weekend. This includes the snacks too. Then make sure that you have the necessary ingredients in advance. It will be easier for you to eat healthy throughout the week. You can even prepare a few meals in advance, especially those you can refrigerate.

Cook with olive oil – Don't use coconut oil or vegetable oil. Extra-virgin olive oil is strongly recommended. Olive oil provides monounsaturated fatty acids that will improve your HDL cholesterol level (the good type). A 2017 study even shows that HDL cholesterol can remove LDL particles from the arteries. Drizzle some olive oil on your food to improve flavor.

Meat-free days – The Med diet is mostly plant-based with some fish. Pulses, beans, and fish will give you all the proteins you need. Meat is only allowed once or twice a weekly. Chicken is better than red meat.

Adopt – Mediterranean flavors might not go precisely with all cuisines. However, you can still adopt many elements. For instance, while preparing something spicy like curry, you can use oils with unsaturated fats. Olive oil is the best. Sunflower and rapeseed oil is better than palm oil or coconut oil.

Antioxidants – Eat vegetables and fruits packed with antioxidants. This will give you pterostilbene, resveratrol, and glutathione. You will get glutathione from onions, garlic, cruciferous vegetables, and spinach. Raspberries and blueberries will provide resveratrol. Oregano, mint, basil and such other herbs will give you other key antioxidants for good health.

Eat wholesome – Pasta, an Italian favorite from the Mediterranean region, also fits into the plan. Prioritize whole-grain options, but you will find grain-free options as well to eliminate having more grains.

Snacking – Have nuts for snacks. Keep a handful of cashews, pistachios, or almonds with you. They are all very satisfying. The Nutrition Journal published a study where it was found that those who replaced chips, cookies, cereal bars, and crackers with almonds ended up adding fewer empty calories, sodium, and added sugar. Nuts will also provide you with essential minerals and fiber.

How to Stay Hydrated. Once you've started and are fully immersed in the Mediterranean diet, you might notice that you've started to feel a little bit weak, and a little bit colder, than you're used to. The Mediterranean diet places an emphasis on trying to cut out as much sodium from your diet as possible, which is very healthy for some of us who already have high sodium levels. Sodium, obviously is found in salt, and so we proceed to cut out salt – and then drink enough water to drain every last drop of sodium from our bodies. When it comes to hydration, the biological mechanisms for keeping us saturated and quenched rely on an equal balance of sodium and potassium. Sodium can be found in your interstitial fluid, and potassium can be found inside our cytoplasm – two sides of one wall. When you drink tons of water, sweat a lot at the gym, or both, your sodium leaves your body in your urine and your sweat.

Potassium, on the other hand, is only really lost through the urine – and even then, it's rare. This means that our bodies almost constantly need a refill on our sodium levels. But if you aren't eating any salt, or drinking any salt, then where are you supposed to get the salt that will help you stay hydrated? Plenty of individuals on the Mediterranean diet choose to manage their hydration through pills, instead of simply adding more salt back into their foods. This is actually a smart route, because sodium taken orally will make it to your blood stream faster.

Meal Preparation and Portion Planning: If you haven't heard of the term "meal prep" before now, it's a beautiful day to learn something that will save you time, stress, and inches on your waistline. Meal prep, short for meal preparation, is a habit that was developed mostly by the body building community in order to accurately track your macronutrients. You will get to go further in-depth about tracking your macronutrients in the next section, but meal prep is one of the most convenient ways to do so. If you work a nine to five job like most of us, you know the struggle of feeding yourself a healthy dinner after work when you're tired, hungry, and just want to go home. When western society started getting more and more fast paced, we developed the fast food restaurant that could serve you from your car. While we all love to indulge in a little junk food now and then, fast food restaurants are marketed more towards routine family use than to a one-off indulgence. If you have kids, you're probably even more familiar with this struggle. Some of the members of the fitness community had finally had enough, and so they developed a way to cook healthy, homemade meals every single week without busting the bank, sacrificing time in the gym, or sacrificing time with your loved ones. The basic idea behind meal prep is that each weekend, you manage your free time around cooking and preparing all of your meals for the upcoming week. While most meal preppers do their grocery shopping and cooking on Sundays, to keep their meals the most fresh, you can choose to cook on a Saturday if that works better with your schedule. Meal prep each week uses one large grocery list of bulk ingredients to get all the supplies you need to make four dinners and four lunches of your choice. This means that you might have to a bit of mental math quadrupling the serving size, but all you have to do is multiply each ingredient by four. Although you don't have to meal prep more than one meal with four portions each week, if you're already in the kitchen, you most likely have cooking time to work on something else. Many body builders even prep their breakfasts and on-the-go snacks during the weekend, to save time and make absolutely sure they know what they're eating. For the average person, meal prepping four dinners alone will already free up a ton of time during the week – for a gym session, perhaps, or more time relaxing with the family. When you cook for meal prep, you're going to be creating one meal in four portions – which can take up a lot of dishes. Investing in some good pots, pans, and skillets will help you work more efficiently in the kitchen, and matching Tupperware are something a good meal prepper can never resist. Once you've cooked your entire four-portion meal in one batch, you can separate out individual matching portions that you will eat throughout the week. Most cooked vegetables and meats can last for up to five days in the refrigerator, but you can feel free to freeze your entrees as well if you need the space. Vegetables that are uncooked normally have three to four days only, but that's why you're only reaching about four days in advance. If you want to keep your meals fresher for longer, you can always look for glass Tupperware with locking seals that can keep freshness in for longer. Each week, you can do repeat this process with new recipes and new ingredients. However, it's worth it to note that if you're someone who likes consistency, meal prepping might be a bit of an adjustment. Meal prep tends to make only one identical dinner meal and one identical lunch meal each week – which means that eaters who like to have a different dinner each night might have their work cut out for them. One of the easiest ways to combat this is by simply making a dinner and a lunch that can be interchanged whenever necessary to create variety. Once you've learned how to meal prep, you will save yourself enough time in the evenings relax, practice some self-care, and really extend your dinner hours to have fun conversation with friends and family. Now, meal preparation isn't just a cool technique to save you time and money – meal prep at its very core was designed to help you manage your weight loss in a convenient way, which is exactly what you need to succeed.

Tracking Your Macronutrients: Wouldn't it be nice if you could have a full nutritional label for each of your home-cooked meals, just to make sure that your numbers are adding up in favor of weight loss? Oddly enough, tracking your macronutrients in order to calculate the nutritional value of each of your meals and portions is as easy as stepping on the scale. Not the scale in your bathroom, however. A food scale! If you've never had a good relationship with your weight and numbers, you might suddenly find that they aren't too bad after all. Food scales are used to measure, well, your food, but there's a slick system of online calculators and fitness applications for you smart phone that can take this number and turn it into magic. When you meal prep each week, keep track of your recipes diligently. Remember how you multiplied each of the ingredients on the list by four to create four servings? You're going to want to remember how much of each vegetable, fruit, grain, nut, and fat you cooked with. While you wait for you meal to finish cooking, find a large enough plastic container to fit all of your meal. Make sure it's clean and dry, and use the empty container to zero out your scale. Once you've finished cooking your entire meal, transfer ALL FOUR PORTIONS into the clean plastic container and take not of the weight. When you use your online calculator or fitness app, you can enter the amount of each ingredient you used to cook the meal, and then the weight of the entire four portions. This will give you an estimate of how many carbohydrates, proteins, and fats are contained within each dish, and how many overall calories your meal comes out to be. Now, you're obviously not going to be consuming all of this at once, and so you will have to divide each number by four in order to get the proper readings. At the end of this process, you will have an almost entirely complete nutritional label for a meal that you made at home, from fresh and healthy ingredients that you know won't make you gain weight. It's one of the many ways that the Mediterranean diet turns something tedious like math and intimidating like scales into a delicious and nutritious way of living a healthier, and happier, life. Speaking of scales, let's talk a little bit about using the caloric estimates on your homemade meals to track your calories, and implicate a deficit, in order to lose more weight than you ever thought possible.

Goal Setting to Meet Your Achievements: On the subject of control, there are a few steps and activities that you should go through before you begin your Mediterranean diet just to make sure that you have clear and realistic goals in mind. Sitting down to set goals before embarking on a totally new diet routine will help you stay focused and committed during your Mediterranean diet. While a Mediterranean diet lifestyle certainly isn't as demanding as some of the crazy diet fads you see today, it can be a struggle to focus on eating natural fruits and vegetables that are more "salt of the Earth" foods than we're used to. You already know that when it comes to weight loss, you shouldn't expect to lose more than one to two pounds per week healthily while you're dieting. You are still welcome to set a weight loss goal with time in mind, but when it comes to the Mediterranean diet, you should set your goals for one month in the future. One month might seem like a long time, but for a diet that's designed to be integrated into your lifestyle, one month will give you a great concept of what you can expect in the year to come. When you set your goals, you should take the time to write down two lists of three bullet points for each goal. The first set should be the three most important reasons to you that you've decided to commit to the Mediterranean diet. The second three should be three helpful tips you have for yourself or ways you can imagine reaching your goal. When you find yourself struggling on days where hunger pangs come more often than usual or the gym didn't go very well, you can look back at your two lists to remind yourself of why you're here in the first place, and the solutions that past you knew future you could handle. Dieting is difficult for all of us, but taking the time to care for yourself and your mental state on a diet can have a huge impact on your happiness (and on your weight loss). One of the next goals you should set for your personal journey on the Mediterranean diet is a meal prepping goal. You're going to be surprised at how easy meal prepping actually is, but a lot of the time you can fall victim to your own laziness after a while. To encourage yourself to continue meal prepping, you should set certain goals each week about new snacks you can prepare,

Cooking multiple dinner meals in one weekend, or trying to meal prep for a dinner party. The more you challenge yourself to learn, the easier your Mediterranean diet will become over time. Nobody likes to get bored, but if you start to slack off with your cooking, you will definitely notice it in your waistline. One of the coolest thing about meal prep is that you'll start to pick up cooking techniques, knife skills, and an intuition about seasonings that you might never have thought possible. Each one of these skills will help speed up your meal prepping process, and, you'll be that much more likely to impress your friends with you skills in the kitchen. The final goal that you should set with yourself as you embark on your Mediterranean diet journey is to be kind to yourself. While this might seem silly, you know the effect that stress can have on your body – and it simply isn't worth it to get worked up and anxious about your weight loss goals. Before you being your diet, promise yourself that you will be gentle, patient, and supportive when you need help – and yet also push yourself when you feel like you aren't progressing quickly enough. Sometimes, we have to be our own coaches, and you shouldn't be afraid to tell yourself the hard truth every now and then. With this nutritional guide at your back, there's no excuse for anything but success if you have the right drive and level of commitment. Now that you've set down come concrete goals that are going to move you forward, you deserve a bit of a treat. Quite literally, let's get into the delicious details of some thirty-minute homemade Mediterranean diet recipes.

Chapter 5: Breakfast

Breakfast Egg on Avocado

Servings: 6

Preparation time: 10 minutes

Cooking Time: 15 minutes

Ingredients: 1 tsp garlic powder

1/2 tsp sea salt

1/4 cup Parmesan cheese (grated or shredded)

1/4 tsp black pepper

3 medium avocados (cut in half, pitted, skin on)

6 medium eggs

Directions: Prepare muffin tins and preheat the oven to 350° F.

To ensure that the egg would fit inside the cavity of the avocado, lightly scrape off 1/3 of the meat.

Place avocado on muffin tin to ensure that it faces with the top up.

Evenly season each avocado with pepper, salt, and garlic powder.

Add one egg on each avocado cavity and garnish tops with cheese.

Pop in the oven and bake until the egg white is set, about 15 minutes.

Serve and enjoy.

Nutritional values per serving: Calories 252; Protein 14 g; Carbs 4 g; Fat 20 g

Breakfast Egg-artichoke Casserole

Servings: 8

Preparation time: 10 minutes

Cooking Time: 35 minutes

Ingredients: 16 large eggs

14 ounce can artichoke hearts, drained

10 ounce box frozen chopped spinach, thawed and drained well

1 cup shredded white cheddar

1 garlic clove, minced

1 teaspoon salt

1/2 cup parmesan cheese

1/2 cup ricotta cheese

1/2 teaspoon dried thyme

1/2 teaspoon crushed red pepper

1/4 cup milk

1/4 cup shaved onion

Directions: Lightly grease a 9x13 inch baking dish with cooking spray and preheat the oven to 350° F.

In a large mixing bowl, add eggs and milk. Mix thoroughly.

With a paper towel, squeeze out the excess moisture from the spinach leaves and add to the bowl of eggs. Into small pieces, break the artichoke hearts and separate the leaves. Add to the bowl of eggs.

Except for the ricotta cheese, add remaining ingredients in the bowl of eggs and mix thoroughly.

Pour egg mixture into the prepared dish.

Evenly add dollops of ricotta cheese on top of the eggs and then pop in the oven.

Bake until eggs are set and doesn't jiggle when shook, about 35 minutes.

Remove from the oven and evenly divide into suggested servings. Enjoy.

Nutritional values per serving: Calories 302; Protein 22.6 g; Carbs 10.8 g; Fat 18.7 g

Brekky Egg-potato Hash

Servings: 2

Preparation time: 10 minutes

Cooking Time: 25 minutes

Ingredients: 1 zucchini, diced

1/2 cup chicken broth

½ pound cooked chicken

1 tablespoon olive oil

4 ounces shrimp

Salt and ground black pepper to taste

1 large sweet potato, diced

2 eggs

1/4 teaspoon cayenne pepper

2 teaspoons garlic powder

1 cup fresh spinach (optional)

Directions: In a skillet, add the olive oil.

Fry the shrimp, cooked chicken and sweet potato for 2 minutes.

Add the cayenne pepper, garlic powder and salt, and toss for 4 minutes.

Add the zucchini and toss for another 3 minutes.

Whisk the eggs in a bowl and add to the skillet.

Season using salt and pepper. Cover with the lid.

Cook for 1 minute and add the chicken broth.

Cover and cook for another 8 minutes on high heat.

Add the spinach and toss for 2 more minutes.

Serve immediately.

Nutritional values per serving: Calories 190; Protein 11.7 g; Carbs 2.9 g; Fat 12.3 g

Dill and Tomato Frittata

Servings: 6

Preparation time: 10 minutes

Cooking Time: 35 minutes

Ingredients: Pepper and salt to taste

1 tsp red pepper flakes

2 garlic cloves, minced

½ cup crumbled goat cheese – optional

2 tbsp fresh chives, chopped

2 tbsp fresh dill, chopped

4 tomatoes, diced

8 eggs, whisked

1 tsp coconut oil

Directions: Grease a 9 inch round baking pan and preheat oven to 325° F.

In a large bowl, mix well all ingredients and pour into prepped pan.

Pop into the oven and bake until middle is cooked through around 30-35 minutes.

Remove from oven and garnish with more chives and dill.

Nutritional values per serving: Calories 149; Protein 13.26 g; Carbs 9.93 g; Fat 10.28 g

Mediterranean Egg White Breakfast Sandwich

Servings: 2

Preparation time: 10 minutes

Cooking Time: 25 minutes

Ingredients: 2 teaspoons butter

Salt and pepper to taste

2 whole grain seeded ciabatta rolls, split, toasted

2 slices Swiss cheese or Muenster cheese

½ cup egg whites, beaten

2 teaspoon minced fresh herbs of your choice

2 tablespoons pesto

For roasted tomatoes:

2 tablespoons extra-virgin olive oil

20 ounces grape tomatoes, halved lengthwise

Kosher salt to taste

Coarsely ground pepper to taste

Directions: Heat a nonstick pan over medium flame.

Toss half the butter and once it starts melting, add half the egg whites.

Sprinkle salt, pepper, and 1 teaspoon of herbs, and cook until the omelet is set. Flip sides and cook the other side for about 30 seconds. Place onto a plate.

Repeat the first steps and make the other omelet.

Meanwhile make the roasted tomatoes as follows: Add tomatoes into a baking dish. Pour oil over it and toss well. Sprinkle with salt and pepper. Spread it evenly in the dish.

Roast in a preheated oven at 400° F for about 20 minutes or charred slightly.

Toast the rolls just before serving.

Spread pesto on the cut part of the rolls.

Place bottom halves of the rolls on individual serving plates. Place an omelet (fold the omelet to fit in) on each.

Place a slice of cheese on each. Cover with top half of the rolls and serve.

Nutritional values per serving: Calories 458; Fat 24 g; Carbs 51 g; Fiber 2 g; Protein 21 g

Mediterranean Breakfast Casserole

Servings: 3

Preparation time: 10 minutes

Cooking Time: 35 minutes

Ingredients: 1 tablespoon olive oil

1 medium potato, peeled, diced

½ pound zucchini, sliced

1 small onion, chopped

2 medium sweet peppers, roasted, peeled

2 Portobello mushroom caps, chopped

1 cup chopped fresh spinach

3.5 ounces light ricotta cheese

3.5 ounces ricotta cheese

3 tablespoons part-skim milk mozzarella cheese, grated

2 tablespoons Pecorino Romano cheese, grated

6 grape tomatoes, sliced into thirds

1 cup egg whites

1 sourdough roll, cubed

Directions: Place onion and potato in a baking dish. Drizzle a teaspoon of oil over it. Toss well and tilt the dish so it spreads evenly.

Bake in a preheated oven at 400° F for about 15 minutes. Transfer on to a baking tray.

Add zucchini into a bowl. Drizzle a teaspoon of oil over it. Toss well and transfer on to the baking tray (with potatoes). Bake for another 40 minutes or until golden brown.

Place a skillet over medium heat. Add 1 teaspoon oil. Once the oil heats, add mushrooms and sauté until soft. Remove from the pan and set aside.

Add 1 teaspoon oil to the same pan and place the pan over heat. Add spinach and cook well, and then turn off the heat when the spinach wilts.

Add ricotta cheese and egg whites into a bowl and whisk well. Set aside.

Add zucchini, onion potato mixture, onion, sour dough roll cubes, and grape tomatoes into a baking dish and mix well.

Pour the ricotta mixture over it. Sprinkle mozzarella cheese and Pecorino Romano cheese.

Bake in a preheated oven at 400° F for 40-50 minutes or until the eggs are cooked as per your desire. Remove the baking dish from the oven and let it cool down for a couple of minutes. Cut it into slices and serve.

Nutritional values per serving: Calories 370.2; Fat 15.7 g; Carbs 34.4 g; Fiber 4.6 g; Protein 25.8 g

Gingerbread Breakfast Quinoa Bake with Banana

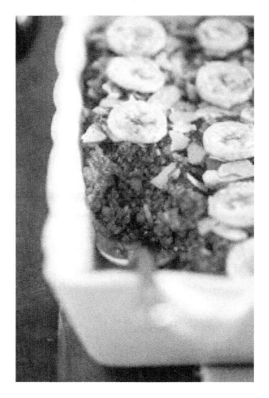

Servings: 4

Preparation time: 10 minutes

Cooking Time: 35 minutes

Ingredients: 3 small ripe bananas, mashed

2 tablespoons pure maple syrup

1 teaspoon raw vanilla extract

½ teaspoon ground cloves

¼ teaspoon salt or to taste

1 ¼ cups unsweetened vanilla almond milk

¼ teaspoon ground allspice

2 tablespoons molasses

½ teaspoon ground ginger

½ tablespoon ground cinnamon

½ cup quinoa, uncooked

2 tablespoons slivered almonds

Directions: Add banana, maple syrup, vanilla, ginger, molasses, salt and all the spices into a casserole dish or baking dish. Mix until well incorporated.

Stir in the quinoa.

Add milk and whisk until well incorporated. Cover and chill overnight.

Remove the dish from the refrigerator and give it a good stir. Cover the dish with foil.

Bake in a preheated oven at 400° F for 40-50 minutes or until dry and cooked through.

Set the oven to broil mode. Scatter the almonds on top. Press lightly to adhere.

Broil for three to four minutes or until almonds are golden brown on top.

Remove the baking dish from the oven and let it cool for five to eight minutes. Cut it into four equal wedges and serve.

Nutritional values per serving: Calories 213; Fat 4 g; Carbs 41 g; Fiber 4 g; Protein 5 g

Egg Muffins with Vegetables and Feta Cheese

Servings: 6

Preparation time: 10 minutes

Cooking time: 15 minutes

Ingredients: 1 cup finely chopped baby spinach

½ cup chopped tomatoes

½ tablespoon chopped fresh oregano

4 eggs, well beaten

½ cup crumbled feta cheese

¼ cup finely chopped onions

¼ cup chopped, pitted Kalamata olives

1 teaspoon sunflower oil + extra to grease

½ cup cooked quinoa

Directions: Grease a 6 counts muffin tin with some oil.

Heat a skillet over medium flame and add oil. Add onions and cook until they turn translucent.

Stir in the tomatoes and cook for a minute. Stir in the spinach and cook until it wilts.

Remove from heat.

Add olives and oregano and mix well.

Add quinoa, salt, and feta cheese into the bowl of beaten eggs and whisk well.

Add the sautéed vegetables and mix well.

Spoon into prepared muffin tins.

Bake in a preheated oven at 350° F for about 25 – 30 minutes or until it is done and the top is light golden brown.

Remove from the oven and cool for a few minutes.

Run a knife around the edges of the muffin and loosen the muffins. Invert onto a plate and serve.

Nutritional values per serving: Calories 114; Fat 7 g; Carb 6 g; Fiber 1 g; Protein 7 g

Mediterranean Breakfast Stir Fry (Melamen)

Servings: 8

Preparation time: 10 minutes

Cooking time: 15 minutes

Ingredients: 3 cups chopped onions

3 cups green bell peppers, chopped

4 large tomatoes, chopped

2 tablespoons extra-virgin olive oil

2 eggs, beaten

Pepper to taste

Salt to taste

Directions: Heat a pan over a high flame. Add oil and then add bell pepper and sauté for a couple of minutes.

Reduce heat, cover and cook for two minutes.

Add onions and stir. Cover and cook for four to five minutes.

Add tomatoes, salt and pepper, stir and cover again. Cook until the tomatoes are soft.

Pour the beaten egg over the veggies in the pan. Do not stir at all. Let it simmer for 50 to 60 seconds.

Serve with pita bread, cucumbers, and low fat feta cheese.

Nutritional values per serving: Calories 108.7; Fat 5.1 g; Carbs 14.3 g; Fiber 3 g; Protein 3.6 g

Mediterranean Pistachios and Fruits with Yogurt

Servings: 6

Preparation time: 10 minutes

Cooking time: 45 minutes

Ingredients: ¾ cup pistachios, unsalted

¼ cup chopped dried apricots

1/8 teaspoon ground or grated nutmeg

1 teaspoon raw sugar

2 tablespoons dried pomegranate seeds or dried cranberries

1/8 teaspoon ground allspice

¼ teaspoon cinnamon

Greek yogurt to serve, as required

Directions: Grease a rimmed baking sheet with cooking spray. Place pistachios on it.

Bake in a preheated oven at 350° F for about seven minutes or until nuts are toasted lightly. Remove from the oven and let it cool.

Transfer the pistachios into a bowl. Add rest of the ingredients except yogurt. Toss well.

Transfer into an airtight container. It can last for a week.

To serve: Serve required quantity of yogurt in serving bowls. Add ¼ cup nut mixture in each bowl and serve.

Nutritional values per serving: ¼ cup without yogurt Calories 116; Fat 7.1 g; Carbs 11 g; Fiber 2.1 g; Protein 3.5 g

Mediterranean Eggs

Servings: 3

Preparation time: 10 minutes

Cooking time: 25 minutes

Ingredients: 1 medium onion, sliced

½ tablespoon extra-virgin olive oil

3 tablespoons firmly packed, julienne cut, sun-dried tomatoes

1.5 ounces crumbled feta cheese

Chopped parsley, to garnish

½ tablespoon butter

2 small cloves garlic, minced

3 large eggs

Kosher salt to taste

Freshly ground pepper to taste

Crusty ciabatta rolls, to serve

Directions: Place a skillet (preferably cast iron) over medium-low heat. Add butter and oil. When the butter melts, stir in the onions and cook until brown. It can take at least 30 minutes. Stir occasionally.

Stir in sun-dried tomatoes and garlic and cook until aromatic. Spread it evenly.

Crack eggs at different spots on top. Scatter feta cheese.

Sprinkle salt and pepper to taste.

Cover and cook until the eggs are cooked. Do not uncover for at least five minutes.

Garnish with parsley and serve over ciabatta rolls.

Nutritional values per serving: Without ciabatta rolls - Calories 183; Fat 11 g; Carbs 11 g; Fiber 1 g; Protein 9 g

Shakshuka

Servings: 6

Preparation time: 10 minutes

Cooking time: 15 minutes

Ingredients: 2 medium onions, chopped

3 cloves garlic, sliced

3 red bell peppers, chopped

½ teaspoon sugar

6 eggs

3 tablespoons olive oil

½ teaspoon spicy harissa peppers

Salt to taste

Pepper to taste

1 ½ cans (15 ounces each) diced tomatoes

Directions: Place a heavy bottomed skillet over medium heat. Add oil and let it heat.

Stir in the onions and cook until onions are tender. Then add the bell peppers and toss for two minutes.

Stir in the garlic and cook for a couple of minutes until aromatic.

Stir in the tomatoes, harissa peppers, salt, pepper, and sugar. Cook for about five to six minutes.

Make six holes in the mixture and crack an egg in each.

Cover with a lid and cook until the eggs are cooked.

Nutritional values per serving: Calories 179; Fat 11 g; Carbs 12 g; Fiber 2 g; Protein 7 g

Berry Breakfast Smoothie

Servings: 1

Preparation time: 10 minutes

Cooking time: 40 minutes

Ingredients: 1 ¼ cups frozen berries of your choice

2 tablespoons milk

1 teaspoon honey

4.4 ounces Greek yogurt

1.8 ounces oats

Directions: Toss all ingredients into a blender and blend on high for a minute. Pour into a glass and serve with crushed ice if desired.

Nutritional values per serving: Calories 295; Fat 5 g; Carbs 44 g; Fiber 7 g; Protein 18 g

Mediterranean Diet Smoothie

Servings: 1

Preparation time: 10 minutes

Cooking time: 45 minutes

Ingredients: 1 cups loosely packed baby spinach

½ banana, sliced, frozen

¼ inch fresh ginger, peeled, sliced

½ small mango, peeled, pitted, chopped

¼ cup skim milk or unsweetened almond milk

½ cup beet juice

Ice cubes, as required

Directions: Toss all ingredients into a blender and blend on high for a minute.

Pour into a glass and serve with crushed ice if desired.

Nutritional values per serving: Calories 168; Fat 1 g; Carbs 39 g; Fiber 5 g; Protein 4 g

Paleo Almond Banana Pancakes

Servings: 3

Preparation time: 10 minutes

Cooking Time: 10 minutes

Ingredients: ¼ cup almond flour

½ teaspoon ground cinnamon

3 eggs

1 banana, mashed

1 tablespoon almond butter

1 teaspoon vanilla extract

1 teaspoon olive oil

Sliced banana to serve

Directions: Whisk the eggs in a mixing bowl until they become fluffy.

In another bowl, mash the banana using a fork and add to the egg mixture.

Add the vanilla, almond butter, cinnamon and almond flour.

Mix into a smooth batter.

Heat the olive oil in a skillet.

Add one spoonful of the batter and fry them on both sides.

Keep doing these steps until you are done with all the batter.

Add some sliced banana on top before serving.

Nutritional values per serving: Calories 306; Protein 14.4 g; Carbs 3.6 g; Fat 26 g

Mediterranean Breakfast Pitas

Servings: 4

Preparation time: 10 minutes

Cooking Time: 30 minutes

Ingredients: 4 Big eggs, at room temperature

Salt

2 Whole wheat pita breads with pockets, cut down the middle

½ cup Hummus (4 ounces)

1 Medium cucumber, meagerly cut into adjusts

2 Medium tomatoes, huge shakers

Handful of new parsley leaves, coarsely hacked

Freshly ground dark pepper

Hot sauce (discretionary)

Directions: 1. Fill a medium pot with water and heat to the point of boiling. Tenderly place your room-temperature eggs in the water and cook for 7 minutes. Channel the water and run the eggs under chilly water to cool. Strip the eggs and cut into ¼ inch-thick cuts. Sprinkle with salt and put in a safe place.

2. Spread within every pita pocket with 2 tablespoons of hummus. Place a couple of cucumber cuts and some diced tomato into every pita. Sprinkle with salt and pepper. Fold 1 cut egg into every pita and sprinkle with parsley and hot sauce (if utilizing).

Nutritional values based on 4 servings (% day by day esteem): Calories 206; Fat 8.3 g (12.8%); Saturated 2.1 g (10.6%); Carbs 22.9 g (7.6%); Fiber 4.9 g; (19.7%); Sugars 3.4 g; Protein 12.0 g (24.1%); Sodium 564.4 mg (23.5%)

Spinach and Artichoke Frittata

Servings: 4 to 6

Preparation time: 5 minutes

Cooking time: 22 minutes to 25 minutes

Ingredients: 10 Big eggs

½ cup Full-fat acrid cream

1 tablespoon Dijon mustard

1 teaspoon Genuine salt

¼ teaspoon Crisply ground dark pepper

1 cup Ground parmesan cheddar (around 3 ounces), divided

2 tablespoons

Olive oil

About 14 ounces

Marinated artichoke hearts, depleted, tapped dry, and quartered

5 ounces Infant spinach (around 5 pressed cups)

2 cloves

Garlic, minced

Directions: 1. Arrange a rack in the broiler and heat to 400° F.

2. Place the eggs, harsh cream, mustard, salt, pepper and ½ cup of the parmesan in a huge bowl and race to consolidate; put in a safe place.

3. Heat the oil in a 10 inch cast iron or broiler safe nonstick skillet over medium heat until gleaming. Include the artichokes in a solitary layer and cook, blending occasionally, until delicately caramelized, 6 to 8 minutes. Include the spinach and garlic, and hurl until the spinach is withered and practically all of the fluid is vanished, around 2 minutes.

4. Spread everything into an even layer. Pour the egg blend over the vegetables. Sprinkle with the staying ½ cup parmesan. Tilt the skillet to ensure the eggs settle uniformly over all the vegetables. Cook undisturbed until the eggs at the edges of the skillet start to set, 2 to 3 minutes.

5. Bake until the eggs are totally set, 12 to 15 minutes. To check, cut a small cut in the focal point of the frittata. If crude eggs run into the cut,

heat for an additional couple of moments. Cool in the search for gold minutes, at that point cut into wedges and serve warm.

Nutritional values based on 6 serving (% day by day esteem):
Calories 316; Fat 25.9 g (39.9%); Saturated 7.8 g (38.9%); Carbs 6.4 g (2.1%); Fiber 2.3 g (9.3%); Sugars 2.1 g; Protein 17.9 g (35.7%); Sodium 565.2 mg (23.6%)

Quinoa Pizza Muffins

Servings: 4

Preparation time: 10 minutes

Cooking Time: 30 minutes

Ingredients: 1 cup uncooked quinoa

2 large eggs

½ medium onion, diced

1 cup diced bell pepper

1 cup shredded mozzarella cheese

1 tbsp dried basil

1 tbsp dried oregano

2 tsp garlic powder

1/8 tsp salt

1 tsp crushed red peppers

½ cup roasted red pepper, chopped

Pizza Sauce, about 1-2 cups

Directions: Preheat oven to 350° F.

Cook quinoa according to directions.

Combine all ingredients (except sauce) into bowl. Mix all ingredients well.

Scoop quinoa pizza mixture into muffin tin evenly. Makes 12 muffins.

Bake for 30 minutes until muffins turn golden in color and the edges are getting crispy.

Top with 1 or 2 tbsp pizza sauce and enjoy!

Nutritional values per serving: Calories 303; Carbs 41.3 g; Protein 21 g; Fat 6.1 g

Rosemary-Walnut Loaf Bread

Servings: 8

Preparation time: 10 minutes

Cooking Time: 45 minutes

Ingredients: ½ cup chopped walnuts

4 tbsp fresh, chopped rosemary

1 1/3 cups lukewarm carbonated water

1 tbsp honey

½ cup extra virgin olive oil

1 tsp apple cider vinegar

3 eggs

5 tsp instant dry yeast granules

1 tsp salt

1 tbsp xanthan gum

¼ cup buttermilk powder

1 cup white rice flour

1 cup tapioca starch

1 cup arrowroot starch

1 ¼ cups all-purpose Bob's Red Mill gluten-free flour mix

Directions: In a large mixing bowl, whisk well eggs. Add 1 cup warm water, honey, olive oil, and vinegar.

While beating continuously, add the rest of the ingredients except for rosemary and walnuts.

Continue beating. If dough is too stiff, add a bit of warm water. Dough should be shaggy and thick.

Then add rosemary and walnuts continue kneading until evenly distributed.

Cover bowl of dough with a clean towel, place in a warm spot, and let it rise for 30 minutes.

Fifteen minutes into rising time, preheat oven to 400° F.

Generously grease with olive oil a 2 quart Dutch oven and preheat inside oven without the lid.

Once dough is done rising, remove pot from oven, and place dough inside. With a wet spatula, spread top of dough evenly in pot.

Brush tops of bread with 2 tbsp of olive oil, cover Dutch oven and bake for 35 to 45 minutes.

Once bread is done, remove from oven. And gently remove bread from pot.

Allow bread to cool at least ten minutes before slicing.

Serve and enjoy.

Nutritional values per serving: Calories 424; Carbs 56.8 g; Protein 7 g; Fat 19 g

Chapter 6: Vegetables

Banana-Coconut Breakfast

Servings: 4

Preparation time: 10 minutes

Cooking Time: 3 minutes

Ingredients: 1 ripe banana

1 cup desiccated coconut

1 cup coconut milk

3 tablespoons raisins, chopped

2 tablespoon ground flax seed

1 teaspoon vanilla

A dash of cinnamon

A dash of nutmeg

Salt to taste

Directions: Place all ingredients in a deep pan.

Allow to simmer for 3 minutes on low heat.

Place in individual containers.

Put a label and store in the fridge.

Allow to thaw at room temperature before heating in the microwave oven.

Nutritional values per serving: Calories per serving 279; Carbs 25.46 g; Protein 6.4 g; Fat 8.8 g; Fiber 5.9g

Basil and Tomato Soup

Servings: 2

Preparation time: 10 minutes

Cooking Time: 25 minutes

Ingredients: Salt and pepper to taste

2 bay leaves

1 ½ cups almond milk, unsweetened

½ tsp raw apple cider vinegar

1/3 cup basil leaves

¼ cup tomato paste

3 cups tomatoes, chopped

1 medium celery stalk, chopped

1 medium carrot, chopped

1 medium garlic clove, minced

½ cup white onion

2 tbsp vegetable broth

Directions: Heat the vegetable broth in a large saucepan over medium heat.

Add the onions and cook for 3 minutes. Add the garlic and cook for another minute.

Add the celery and carrots and cook for 1 minute.

Mix in the tomatoes and bring to a boil. Simmer for 15 minutes.

Add the almond milk, basil and bay leaves. Season with salt and pepper to taste.

Nutritional values per serving: Calories 213; Carbs 42 g; Protein 6.9 g; Fat 3.9 g

Butternut Squash Hummus

Servings: 8

Preparation time: 10 minutes

Cooking Time: 15 minutes

Ingredients: 2 pounds butternut squash, seeded and peeled

1 tablespoon olive oil

¼ cup tahini

2 tablespoons lemon juice

2 cloves of garlic, minced

Salt and pepper to taste

Directions: Heat the oven to 300° F.

Coat the butternut squash with olive oil.

Place in a baking dish and bake for 15 minutes in the oven.

Once the squash is cooked, place in a food processor together with the rest of the ingredients.

Pulse until smooth.

Place in individual containers.

Put a label and store in the fridge.

Allow to warm at room temperature before heating in the microwave oven.

Serve with carrots or celery sticks.

Nutritional values per serving: Calories 115; Carbs 15.8 g; Protein 2.5 g; Fat 5.8 g; Fiber 6.7 g

Cajun Jambalaya Soup

Servings: 6

Preparation time: 10 minutes

Cooking Time: 6 hours

Ingredients: ¼ cup Frank's red hot sauce

3 tbsp Cajun seasoning

2 cups okra

½ head of cauliflower

1 pkg spicy Andouille sausages

4 oz chicken, diced

1 lb. large shrimps, raw and deveined

2 bay leaves

2 cloves garlic, diced

1 large can organic diced tomatoes

1 large onion, chopped

4 pepper

5 cups chicken stock

Directions: In slow cooker, place the bay leaves, red hot sauce, Cajun seasoning, chicken, garlic, onions, and peppers.

Set slow cooker on low and cook for 5 ½ hours.

Then add sausages cook for 10 minutes.

Meanwhile, pulse cauliflower in food processor to make cauliflower rice.

Add cauliflower rice into slow cooker. Cook for 20 minutes.

Serve and enjoy.

Nutritional values per serving: Calories 155; Carbs 13.9 g; Protein 17.4 g; Fat 3.8 g

Portobello Mushroom Pizza

Servings: 4

Preparation time: 10 minutes

Cooking Time: 12 minutes

Ingredients: ½ teaspoon red pepper flakes

A handful of fresh basil, chopped

1 can black olives, chopped

1 medium onion, chopped

1 green pepper, chopped

¼ cup chopped roasted yellow peppers

½ cup prepared nut cheese, shredded

2 cups prepared gluten-free pizza sauce

8 Portobello mushrooms, cleaned and stems removed

Directions: Preheat the oven toaster.

Take a baking sheet and grease it. Set aside.

Place the Portobello mushroom cap-side down and spoon 2 tablespoon of packaged pizza sauce on the underside of each cap. Add nut cheese and top with the remaining ingredients.

Broil for 12 minutes or until the toppings are wilted.

Nutritional values per serving: Calories 578; Carbs 73 g; Protein 24.4 g; Fat 22.4 g

Roasted Root Veggies

Servings: 6

Preparation time: 10 minutes

Cooking Time: 1 hour and 30 minutes

Ingredients: 2 tbsp olive oil

1 head garlic, cloves separated and peeled

1 large turnip, peeled and cut into ½ inch pieces

1 medium sized red onion, cut into ½ inch pieces

1 ½ lbs. beets, trimmed but not peeled, scrubbed and cut into ½ inch pieces

1 ½ lbs. Yukon gold potatoes, unpeeled, cut into ½ inch pieces

2 ½ lbs. butternut squash, peeled, seeded, cut into ½ inch pieces

Directions: Grease 2 rimmed and large baking sheets. Preheat oven to 425° F.

In a large bowl, mix all ingredients thoroughly.

Into the two baking sheets, evenly divide the root vegetables, spread in one layer.

Season generously with pepper and salt.

Pop into the oven and roast for 1 hour and 15 minute or until golden brown and tender.

Remove from oven and let it cool for at least 15 minutes before serving.

Nutritional values per serving: Calories 298; Carbs 61.1 g; Protein: 7.4 g; Fat: 5 g

Amazingly Good Parsley Tabbouleh

Servings: 4

Preparation time: 10 minutes

Cooking Time: 15 minutes

Ingredients: ¼ cup chopped fresh mint

¼ cup lemon juice

¼ tsp salt

½ cup bulgur

½ tsp minced garlic

1 cup water

1 small cucumber, peeled, seeded and diced

2 cups finely chopped flat-leaf parsley

2 tbsp extra virgin olive oil

2 tomatoes, diced

4 scallions, thinly sliced

Pepper to taste

Directions: Cook bulgur according to package instructions. Drain and set aside to cool for at least 15 minutes.

In a small bowl, mix pepper, salt, garlic, oil, and lemon juice.

Transfer bulgur into a large salad bowl and mix in scallions, cucumber, tomatoes, mint, and parsley.

Pour in dressing and toss well to coat.

Place bowl in ref until chilled before serving.

Nutritional values per serving: Calories 134.8; Carbs 13 g; Protein 7.2 g; Fat 6 g

Appetizing Mushroom Lasagna

Servings: 8

Preparation time: 10 minutes

Cooking Time: 75 minutes

Ingredients: ½ cup grated Parmigiano Reggiano cheese

No boil lasagna noodles

Cooking spray

¼ cup all-purpose flour

3 cups reduced fat milk, divided

2 tbsp chopped fresh chives, divided

1/3 cup less fat cream cheese

½ cup white wine

6 garlic cloves, minced and divided

1 ½ tbsp. Chopped fresh thyme

½ tsp freshly ground black pepper, divided

1 tsp salt, divided

1 package 4 oz pre-sliced exotic mushroom blend

1 package 8oz pre-sliced cremini mushrooms

1 ¼ cups chopped shallots

2 tbsp olive oil, divided

1 tbsp butter

1 oz dried porcini mushrooms

1 cup boiling water

Directions: For 30 minutes, submerge porcini in 1 cup boiling hot water. With a sieve, strain mushroom and reserve liquid.

Over medium high fire, melt butter on a fry pan. Mix in 2 tbsp oil and for three minutes fry shallots. Add ¼ tsp pepper, ½ tsp salt, exotic mushrooms and cremini, cook for six minutes. Stir in 3 garlic cloves and thyme, cook for a minute. Bring to a boil as you pour wine by increasing fire to high and cook until liquid evaporates around a minute. Turn off fire and stir in porcini mushrooms, 1 tbsp chives and cream cheese. Mix well.

On medium high fire, place a separate medium sized pan with 1 tbsp oil. Sauté for half a minute 3 garlic cloves. Then bring to a boil as you pour 2 ¾ cups milk and reserved porcini liquid. Season with remaining pepper and salt. In a separate bowl, whisk together flour and ¼ cup milk and pour into pan. Stir constantly and cook until mixture thickens.

In a greased rectangular glass dish, pour and spread ½ cup of sauce, top with lasagna, top with half of mushroom mixture and another layer of lasagna. Repeat the layering process and instead of lasagna layer, end with the mushroom mixture and cover with cheese.

For 45 minutes, bake the lasagna in a preheated 350° F oven. Garnish with chives before serving.

Nutritional values per serving: Calories 268; Carbs 29.6 g; Protein 10.2 g; Fat 12.6 g

Artichokes, Olives & Tuna Pasta

Servings: 4

Preparation time: 10 minutes

Cooking Time: 15 minutes

Ingredients: ¼ cup chopped fresh basil

¼ cup chopped green olives

¼ tsp freshly ground pepper

½ cup white wine

½ tsp salt, divided

1 10 oz package frozen artichoke hearts, thawed and squeezed dry

2 cups grape tomatoes, halved

2 tbsp lemon juice

2 tsp chopped fresh rosemary

2 tsp freshly grated lemon zest

3 cloves garlic, minced

4 tbsp extra virgin olive oil, divided

6 oz whole wheat penne pasta

8 oz tuna steak, cut into 3 pieces

Directions: Cook penne pasta according to package instructions. Drain and set aside.

Preheat grill to medium high.

In bowl, toss and mix ¼ tsp pepper, ¼ tsp salt, 1 tsp rosemary, lemon zest, 1 tbsp oil and tuna pieces.

Grill tuna for 3 minutes per side. Allow to cool and flake into bite sized pieces. On medium fire, place a large nonstick saucepan and heat 3 tbsp oil.

Sauté remaining rosemary, garlic olives, and artichoke hearts for 4 minutes Add wine and tomatoes, bring to a boil and cook for 3 minutes while stirring once in a while. Add remaining salt, lemon juice, tuna pieces and pasta. Cook until heated through.

To serve, garnish with basil and enjoy.

Nutritional values per serving: Calories 127.6; Carbs 13 g; Protein 7.2 g; Fat 5.2 g

Chapter 7: Poultry and meat

Lemon Garlic Chicken

Servings: 6

Preparation time: 10 minutes

Cooking Time: 1 hour and 20 minutes

Ingredients: 6 chicken breast fillets

3 tablespoons olive oil

1 tablespoon lemon juice

3 cloves garlic, crushed and minced

2 teaspoon dried parsley

Directions: Marinate the chicken breast fillets in a mixture of olive oil, lemon juice, garlic, parsley, and a pinch of salt and pepper.

Let sit for 1 hour covered in the refrigerator.

Press the sauté setting in the Instant Pot.

Pour in the vegetable oil.

Cook the chicken for 5 minutes per side or until fully cooked.

Serving Suggestion: Serve with rice or salad.

Tip: You can also slice the chicken before cooking.

Nutritional values per serving: Calories 341; Total Fat 17.9 g; Saturated Fat 4 g; Cholesterol 130 mg; Sodium 127 mg; Total Carbohydrate 0.7 g; Dietary Fiber 0.1 g; Total Sugars 0.1 g; Protein 42.4 g; Potassium 368 mg

Chicken & Rice

Servings: 8

Preparation time: 10 minutes

Cooking Time: 50 minutes

Ingredients: 1 whole chicken, sliced into smaller pieces.

2 tablespoons dry Greek seasoning

1 1/2 cups long grain white rice

1 cup chopped parsley

Directions: Coat the chicken with the seasoning mix.

Add 2 cups of water to the Instant Pot.

Add the chicken inside.

Seal the pot.

Choose manual mode.

Cook at high pressure for 30 minutes.

Release the pressure naturally.

Lift the chicken and place on a baking sheet.

Bake in the oven for 5 minutes or until skin is crispy.

While waiting, strain the broth from the Instant Pot to remove the chicken residue.

Add the rice.

Seal the pot.

Set it to rice function.

Fluff the rice and serve with the chicken.

Nutritional values per serving: Calories 412; Total Fat 11.2 g; Saturated Fat 3.1 g; Cholesterol 130 mg; Sodium 249 mg; Total Carbohydrate 29.3 g; Dietary Fiber 0.7 g; Total Sugars 0.1 g; Protein 45.1 g; Potassium 450 mg

Chicken Shawarma

Servings: 8

Preparation time: 10 minutes

Cooking Time: 30 minutes

Ingredients: 2 lb. chicken breast, sliced into strips

1 teaspoon paprika

1 teaspoon ground cumin

1/4 teaspoon granulated garlic

1/2 teaspoon turmeric

1/4 teaspoon ground allspice

Directions: Season the chicken with the spices, and a little salt and pepper.

Pour 1 cup chicken broth to the pot.

Seal the pot.

Choose poultry setting.

Cook for 15 minutes.

Release the pressure naturally.

Serving Suggestion: Serve with roasted sweet potatoes.

Nutritional values per serving: Calories 132; Total Fat 3 g; Saturated Fat 0 g; Cholesterol 73 mg; Sodium 58 mg; Total Carbohydrate 0.5 g; Dietary Fiber 0.2 g; Total Sugars 0.1 g; Protein 24.2 g; Potassium 435 mg

Mediterranean Chicken

*Servings:*6

Preparation time: 10 minutes

Cooking time: 10 minutes

Ingredients: 2 lb. chicken breast fillet, sliced into strips

Wine mixture (1/4 cup white wine mixed with 3 tablespoons red wine)

2 tablespoons light brown sugar

1 1/2 teaspoons dried oregano

6 garlic cloves, chopped

Directions: Pour in the wine mixture to the Instant Pot.

Stir in the rest of the ingredients.

Toss the chicken to coat evenly.

Seal the pot.

Set it to high pressure.

Cook for 10 minutes.

Release the pressure naturally.

Serving Suggestion: Serve with white rice.

Nutritional values per serving: Calories 304; Total Fat 11.3 g; Saturated Fat 3.1 g; Cholesterol 135 mg; Sodium 131mg; Total Carbohydrate 4.2 g; Dietary Fiber 0.2 g; Total Sugars 3 g; Protein 44 g; Potassium 390 mg

Lime Chicken with Black Beans

Servings: 8

Preparation time: 10 minutes

Cooking Time: 30 minutes

Ingredients: 8 chicken thighs (boneless and skinless)

3 tablespoons lime juice

1 cup black beans

1 cup canned tomatoes

4 teaspoons garlic powder

Directions: Marinate the chicken in a mixture of lime juice and garlic powder.

Add the chicken to the Instant Pot.

Pour the tomatoes on top of the chicken.

Seal the pot.

Set it to manual.

Cook at high pressure for 10 minutes.

Release the pressure naturally.

Stir in the black beans.

Press sauté to simmer until black beans are cooked.

Serving Suggestion: Serve with rice or salad.

Tip: You can also add dried herbs to the recipe.

Nutritional values per serving: Calories 370; Total Fat 11.2 g; Saturated Fat 3.1 g; Cholesterol 130 mg; Sodium 128mg; Total Carbohydrate 17.5 g; Dietary Fiber 4.1 g; Total Sugars 1.5 g; Protein 47.9 g; Potassium 790 mg

Mediterranean Chicken Wings

Servings: 4

Preparation time: 10 minutes

Cooking Time: 1 hour and 20 minutes

Ingredients: 8 chicken wings

1 tablespoon garlic puree

2 tablespoons mixed dried herbs (tarragon, oregano and basil)

1 tablespoon chicken seasoning

Directions: In a bowl, mix the garlic puree, herbs and seasoning.

Marinate the chicken in this mixture for 1 hour.

Add 1 tablespoon of coconut oil into the Instant Pot.

Set it to sauté.

Cook the chicken until brown on both sides.

Remove and set aside.

Add 1 cup of water to the pot.

Place steamer basket inside.

Put the chicken on top of the basket.

Seal the pot.

Set it to manual and cook at high pressure for 10 minutes.

Release the pressure naturally.

Serving Suggestion: Serve with fresh green salad.

Tip: You can also use minced garlic in place of garlic puree.

Nutritional values per serving: Calories 280; Total Fat 11.2 g; Saturated Fat 3 g; Cholesterol 130 mg; Sodium 135 mg; Total Carbohydrate 0 g; Dietary Fiber 0 g; Total Sugars 0 g; Protein 42.2 g; Potassium 355 mg

Honey Balsamic Chicken

Servings: 10

Preparation time: 10 minutes

Cooking Time: 1 hour

Ingredients: 1/4 cup honey

1/2 cup balsamic vinegar

1/4 cup soy sauce

2 cloves garlic minced

10 chicken drumsticks

Directions: Mix the honey, vinegar, soy sauce and garlic in a bowl.

Marinate the chicken in the sauce for 30 minutes.

Cover the pot.

Set it to manual.

Cook at high pressure for 10 minutes.

Release the pressure quickly.

Choose the sauté button to thicken the sauce.

Serving Suggestion: Garnish with lemon wedges.

Tip: You can also use chicken wings or other chicken parts for this recipe.

Nutritional values per serving: Calories 184; Total Fat 4.4 g; Saturated Fat 1.2 g; Cholesterol 67 mg; Sodium 662 mg; Total Carbohydrate 13 g; Dietary Fiber 0.1 g; Total Sugars 11.9 g; Protein 21.9 g; Potassium 202 mg

Beef Corn Chili

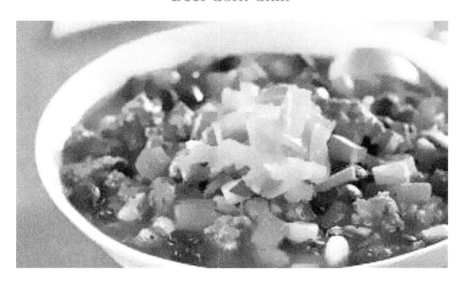

Servings: 8

Preparation Time: 8-10 minutes

Cooking Time: 30 minutes

Ingredients: 2 small onions, chopped (finely)

¼ cup canned corn

1 tablespoon oil

10 ounces lean ground beef

2 small chili peppers, diced

Directions: Take your instant pot and place over dry kitchen surface; open its top lid and switch it on. Press "SAUTE". In its Cooking pot, add and heat the oil. Add the onions, chili pepper, and beef; cook for 2-3 minutes until turn translucent and softened. Add the 3 cups water in the

Cooking pot; combine to mix well. Close its top lid and make sure that its valve it closed to avoid spilling.

Press "MEAT/STEW". Adjust the timer to 20 minutes.

Press will slowly build up; let the added ingredients to cook until the timer indicates zero.

Press "CANCEL". Now press "NPR" for natural release pressure. Instant pot will gradually release pressure for about 8-10 minutes. Open the top lid; transfer the cooked recipe in serving plates.

Serve the recipe warm.

Nutritional values per serving: Calories 94; Protein 7 g; Fat 5 g; Carbs 2 g

Balsamic Beef Dish

Servings: 8

Preparation Time: 5 minutes

Cooking Time: 55 minutes

Ingredients: 3 pounds chuck roast

3 cloves garlic, thinly sliced

1 tablespoon oil

1 teaspoon flavored vinegar

½ teaspoon pepper

½ teaspoon rosemary

1 tablespoon butter

½ teaspoon thyme

¼ cup balsamic vinegar

1 cup beef broth

Directions: Cut slits in the roast and stuff garlic slices all over.

Take a bowl and add flavored vinegar, rosemary, pepper, thyme and rub the mixture over the roast.

Set your pot to sauté mode and add oil, allow the oil to heat up.

Add roast and brown both sides (5 minutes each side).

Take the roast out and keep it on the side.

Add butter, broth, balsamic vinegar and deglaze the pot.

Transfer the roast back and lock up the lid, cook on HIGH pressure for 40 minutes.

Perform a quick release.

Remove the lid and serve!

Nutritional values per serving: Calories 393; Protein 37 g; Fat 15 g; Carbs 25 g

Soy Sauce Beef Roast

Servings: 2-3

Preparation Time: 5-8 minutes

Cooking Time: 35 minutes

Ingredients: ½ teaspoon beef bouillon

1 ½ teaspoon rosemary

½ teaspoon minced garlic

2 pounds roast beef

1/3 cup soy sauce

Directions: Mix the soy sauce, bouillon, rosemary, and garlic together in a mixing bowl.

Place your instant pot over as dry kitchen platform. Open the top lid and plug it on.

Add the roast, bowl mix and enough water to cover the roast; gently stir to mix well.

Properly close the top lid; make sure that the safety valve is properly locked.

Press "MEAT/STEW" Cooking function; set pressure level to "HIGH" and set the Cooking time to 35 minutes.

Allow the pressure to build to cook the ingredients.

After Cooking time is over press "CANCEL" setting. Find and press "NPR" Cooking function. This setting is for the natural release of inside pressure, and it takes around 10 minutes to slowly release pressure.

Slowly open the lid, take out the cooked meat and shred it.

Add the shredded meat back in the potting mix and stir to mix well.

Take out the cooked recipe in serving containers. Serve warm.

Nutritional values per serving: Calories 423; Protein 21 g; Fat 14 g; Carbs12 g

Rosemary Beef Chuck Roast

Servings: 5-6

Preparation Time: 5 minutes

Cooking Time: 45 minutes

Ingredients: 3 pounds chuck beef roast

3 garlic cloves

¼ cup balsamic vinegar

1 sprig fresh rosemary

1 sprig fresh thyme

1 cup of water

1 tablespoon vegetable oil

Salt and pepper to taste

Directions: Cut slices in the beef roast and place the garlic cloves in them.

Coat the roast with the herbs, black pepper, and salt.

Preheat your instant pot using the sauté setting and add the oil.

When warmed, add the beef roast and stir-cook until browned on all sides.

Add the remaining ingredients; stir gently. Seal the lid and cook on high pressure for 40 minutes using the manual setting. Let the pressure release naturally, about 10 minutes. Uncover the instant pot; transfer the beef roast the serving plates, slice and serve.

Nutritional values per serving: Calories 542; Protein 55.2 g; Fat 11.2 g; Carbs 8.7 g

Pork Chops and Tomato Sauce

Servings: 4

Preparation Time: 10 minutes

Cooking Time: 20 minutes

Ingredients: 4 pork chops, boneless

1 tablespoon soy sauce

¼ teaspoon sesame oil

1 and ½ cups tomato paste

1 yellow onion

8 mushrooms, sliced

Directions: In a bowl, mix pork chops with soy sauce and sesame oil, toss and leave aside for 10 minutes.

Set your instant pot on sauté mode, add pork chops and brown them for 5 minutes on each side.

Add onion, stir and cook for 1-2 minutes more.

Add tomato paste and mushrooms, toss, cover and cook on high for 8-9 minutes.

Divide everything between plates and serve.

Enjoy!

Nutritional values per serving: Calories 300; Protein 4 g; Fat 7 g; Carbs 18 g

Pork Potato

Servings: 4

Preparation Time: 8-10 minutes

Cooking Time: 25 minutes

Ingredients: 10 ounces pork neck, fat remove and make small pieces

1 medium sweet potato, chopped

1 tablespoon oil

3 cups beef stock, Low – sodium

1 onion, chopped (finely)

Directions: Take your pot and place over dry kitchen surface; open its top lid and switch it on.

Press "sauté". Grease the pot with some Cooking oil.

Add the onions; cook for 2 minutes until turn translucent and softened.

Add the meat; stir-cook for 4-5 minutes to evenly brown.

Mix in the stock and potatoes.

Close its top lid and make sure that its valve it closed to avoid spillage.

Press "Manual". Adjust the timer to 20 minutes.

Pressure will slowly build up; let the added ingredients to cook until the timer indicates zero.

Press "CANCEL". Now press "NPR" for natural release pressure. Instant pot will gradually release pressure for about 8-10 minutes.

Open the top lid transfer the cooked recipe in serving plates.

Serve the recipe warm.

Nutritional values per serving: Calories 278; Protein 18 g; Fat 18 g; Carbs 12 g

Coffee Flavored Pork Ribs

Servings: 4

Preparation Time: 3 minutes

Cooking Time: 40 minutes

Ingredients: 1 rack baby back ribs

2 teaspoons sesame oil

3 tablespoons oyster sauce

1 teaspoon salt

1 teaspoon sugar

1 cup of water

A ½ cup of liquid smoke

2 tablespoons instant coffee powder

Directions: Add the listed ingredients to the pot.

Lock the lid and cook on MEAT/STEW mode for 40 minutes.

Release the pressure naturally over 10 minutes.

Serve and enjoy!

Nutritional values per serving: Calories 898; Protein 77 g; Fat 63 g; Carbs 4 g

Tomato Pork Paste

Servings: 4

Preparation Time: 5-8 minutes

Cooking Time: 15 minutes

Ingredients: 2 cups tomato puree

1 tablespoon red wine

1 pound lean ground pork

8-10 ounce pack paste of your choice, uncooked

Salt and black pepper to taste

1 tablespoon vegetable oil

Directions: Season the pork with black pepper and salt.

Place your instant pot over a dry kitchen platform. Open the top lid and plug it on.

Press "SAUTE" Cooking function; add the oil and heat it.

In the pot, add the ground meat; stir-cook using wooden spatula until turns evenly brown for 8-10 minutes.

Add the wine. Cook for 1-2 minutes.

Add the ingredients; gently stir to mix well.

Properly close the top lid; make sure that the safety valve is properly locked.

Press "MEAT/STEW" Cooking function; set pressure level to "HIGH" and set the Cooking time to 6 minutes.

Allow the pressure to build to cook the ingredients.

After Cooking time is over press "CANCEL" setting. Find and press "NPR" Cooking function. This setting is for the natural release of inside pressure, and it takes around 10 minutes to slowly release pressure.

Slowly open the lid, take out the cooked recipe in serving containers. Serve warm.

Nutritional values per serving: Calories 423; Protein 36 g; Fat 34 g; Carbs 14 g

Garlic Pulled Pork

Servings: 12

Preparation Time: 5 minutes

Cooking Time: 95-100 minutes

Ingredients: 4 pounds pork shoulder, boneless and cut into 3 pieces

2 tablespoons soy sauce

2 tablespoons brown sugar

1 cup chicken broth

10 cloves garlic, finely chopped

2 tablespoons butter, melted at room temperature

Directions: In a mixing bowl, combine the broth, soy sauce, and brown sugar. Add the garlic and stir to combine. Preheat your instant pot using the sauté setting and add the butter.

When warmed, add the pork pieces and stir-cook until browned on all sides.

Add the soy mix; stir gently.

Seal the lid and cook on high pressure for 90 minutes using the manual setting.

Let the pressure release naturally, about 10 minutes.

Uncover the instant pot; take out the meat and shred it using a fork.

Return the shredded meat to the instant pot and stir the mixture well.

Transfer to serving plates and serve.

Nutritional values per serving: Calories 142; Protein 11.2 g; Fat 8.2 g; Carbs 3.5 g

Simple Lamb Ribs and Sauce

Servings: 2

Preparation Time: 10 minutes

Cooking Time: 30 minutes

Ingredients: 4 lamb ribs

1 carrot, chopped

6 ounces veggie stock

1 tablespoon olive oil

1 tablespoon white flour

Directions: Set your instant pot on sauté mode, add the oil, heat it up, add lamb and brown it for a few minutes on all sides.

Add flour, carrot and stock stir, cover the pot, and cook on high for 20 minutes.

Serve lamb with carrots on the side and Cooking juice drizzled all over.

Enjoy!

Nutritional values per serving: Calories 200; Protein 25 g; Fat 4 g; Carbs 14 g

Rosemary Lamb

Servings: 7-8

Preparation Time: 8-10 minutes

Cooking Time: 50 minutes

Ingredients: 2 onions, chopped

2 rosemary sprigs

3 cups beef broth, low-sodium

2 lamb shanks, about 1 pound each

2 bay leaves

Directions: Take your instant pot and place over dry kitchen surface; open its top lid and switch it on.

Press "SAUTE". Grease the pot with some Cooking oil.

Add the meat; stir-cook for 4-5 minutes to evenly brown. Set aside.

Add the onions; cook for 3-4 minutes until turn translucent and softened.

Add the meat and pour in the broth.

Add the remaining ingredients and stir well.

Close its top and make sure that its valve it closed to avoid spillage.

Press "MANUAL". Adjust the timer to 40 minutes.

Pressure will slowly build up; let the added ingredients to cook until the timer indicates zero.

Press "CANCEL". Now press "QPR" to quickly release pressure.

Open the top lid; transfer the cooked recipe in serving plates.

Remove the rosemary spring and bay leaves. Serve the recipe warm.

Nutritional values per serving: Calories 318; Protein 37 g; Fat 17 g; Carbs 3 g

Lamb Shanks Curry

Servings: 5

Preparation Time: 10 minutes

Cooking Time: 45 minutes

Ingredients: 3 pounds lamb shanks

Kosher flavored vinegar

Fresh ground black pepper

2 tablespoons ghee

2 medium carrots, roughly chopped

2 celery, chopped

1 large onion, chopped

1 tablespoon tomato paste

3 cloves, peeled and smashed

1 cup bone broth

1 teaspoon red boat fish sauce

1 tablespoon vinegar

Directions: Season the shanks with pepper and flavored vinegar. Set your pot to sauté mode and add ghee, allow the ghee to melt and heat up.

Add shanks and cook for 8-10 minutes until a nice brown texture appears.

In the meantime, chop the vegetables.

Once you have a nice brown texture on your lamb, remove it from the instant pot and keep it on the side.

Add vegetable and season with flavored vinegar and pepper.

Add a tablespoon of ghee and mix.

Add vegetables, garlic clove, and tomato paste and give it a nice stir.

Add shanks and pour broth, vinegar, fish sauce. Sprinkle a bit of pepper and lock up the lid. Cook on HIGH pressure naturally over 45 minutes. Release the pressure naturally over 10 minutes.

Serve the shanks and enjoy!

Nutritional values per serving: Calories 377; Protein 13 g; Fat 16 g; Carbs 10 g

Lamb Coconut Curry

Servings: 4-5

Preparation Time: 5-8 minutes

Cooking Time: 15 minutes

Ingredients: 2 pounds lamb, diced

A small bunch of lemongrass stalks, trimmed and diced

4 tablespoons minced chili

1 inch pieces ginger root, chopped

1 cup of coconut milk

Directions: Blend the lemongrass, ginger, and chili in a blender to make a paste. Place your instant pot over a dry kitchen platform. Open the top lid and plug it on.

Add the paste, lamb, and coconut milk; gently stir to mix well.

Properly close the top lid; make sure that the safety valve is properly locked.

Press "MEAT/STEW" Cooking function; set pressure level to "HIGH" and set the Cooking time to 15 minutes.

Allow the pressure to build to cook the ingredients.

After Cooking time is over press "CANCEL" setting. Find and press "QPR" Cooking function. This setting is for quick release of inside pressure.

Slowly open the lid, take out the cooked recipe in serving containers. Serve warm.

Nutritional values per serving: Calories 524; Protein 31 g; Fat 19 g; Carbs 28g

Chapter 8: Lunch

Crispy Black-Eyed Peas

Servings: 6

Preparation Time: 10 minutes

Cooking Time: 15 minutes

Ingredients: 15 ounces black-eyed peas

1/8 teaspoon chipotle chili powder

¼ teaspoon salt

½ teaspoon chili powder

1/8 teaspoon black pepper

Directions: Rinse the beans well with running water then set aside. In a large bowl, mix the spices until well combined. Add the peas to spices and mix. Place the peas in the wire basket and cook for 10 minutes at 360° F. Serve and enjoy!

Nutritional values per serving: Calories 262; Total Fat 9.4 g; Carbs 8.6 g; Protein 9.2 g

Lemony Green Beans

Servings: 4

Preparation Time: 12 minutes

Cooking Time: 15 minutes

Ingredients: 1 lb. green beans washed and destemmed

Sea salt and black pepper to taste

1 lemon

¼ teaspoon extra virgin olive oil

Directions: Preheat your air fryer to 400° F. Place the green beans in the air fryer basket. Squeeze lemon over beans and season with salt and pepper. Cover ingredients with oil and toss well. Cook green beans for 12 minutes and serve!

Nutritional values per serving: Calories 263: Total Fat 9.2 g; Carbs 8.6 g; Protein 8.7 g

Roasted Orange Cauliflower

Servings: 2

Preparation Time: 20 minutes

Cooking Time: 15 minutes

Ingredients: 1 head cauliflower

½ lemon, juiced

½ tablespoon olive oil

1 teaspoon curry powder

Sea salt and black pepper to taste

Directions: Prepare your cauliflower by washing and removing the leaves and core. Slice it into florets of comparable size. Grease your air fryer with oil and preheat it for 2 minutes at 390° F. Combine fresh lemon juice and curry powder, add the cauliflower florets and stir. Use salt and pepper as seasoning and stir again. Cook for 20 minutes and serve warm.

Eggplant Parmesan Panini

Servings: 2

Preparation Time: 25 minutes

Cooking Time: 15 minutes

Ingredients: 1 medium eggplant, cut into ½ inch slices

½ cup mayonnaise

2 tablespoons milk

Black pepper to taste

½ teaspoon garlic powder

½ teaspoon onion powder

1 tablespoon dried parsley

½ teaspoon Italian seasoning

½ cup breadcrumbs

Sea salt to taste

Fresh basil, chopped for garnishing

¾ cup tomato sauce

2 tablespoons parmesan, grated cheese

2 cups grated mozzarella cheese

2 tablespoons olive oil

4 slices artisan Italian bread

Cooking spray

Directions: Cover both sides of eggplant with salt. Place them between sheets of paper towels. Set aside for 30 minutes to get rid of excess moisture. In a mixing bowl, combine Italian seasoning, breadcrumbs, parsley, onion powder, garlic powder and season with salt and pepper. In another small bowl, whisk mayonnaise and milk until smooth.

Preheat your air fryer to 400° F. Remove the excess salt from eggplant slices. Cover both sides of eggplant with mayonnaise mixture. Press the eggplant slices into the breadcrumb mixture. Use cooking spray on both sides of eggplant slices. Air fry slices in batches for 15 minutes, turning over when halfway done. Each bread slice must be greased with olive oil. On a cutting board, place two slices of bread with oiled sides down. Layer mozzarella cheese and grated parmesan cheese. Place eggplant on cheese. Cover with tomato sauce and add remaining mozzarella and parmesan cheeses. Garnish with chopped fresh basil. Put the second slice of bread oiled side up on top. Take preheated Panini press and place sandwiches on it. Close the lid and cook for 10 minutes. Slice panini into halves and serve.

Nutritional values per serving: Calories 267; Total Fat 11.3 g; Carbs 8.7 g; Protein 8.5 g

Spinach Samosa

Servings: 2

Preparation Time: 15 minutes

Cooking Time: 15 minutes

Ingredients: 1 ½ cups of almond flour

½ teaspoon baking soda

1 teaspoon garam masala

1 teaspoon coriander, chopped

¼ cup green peas

½ teaspoon sesame seeds

¼ cup potatoes, boiled, small chunks

2 tablespoons olive oil

¾ cup boiled and blended spinach puree

Salt and chili powder to taste

Directions: In a bowl, mix baking soda, salt, and flour to make the dough. Add 1 tablespoon of oil. Add the spinach puree and mix until the dough is smooth. Place in fridge for 20 minutes. In the pan add one tablespoon of oil, then add potatoes, peas and cook for 5 minutes. Add the sesame seeds, garam masala, coriander, and stir. Knead the dough and make the small ball using a rolling pin. Form balls, make into cone shapes, which are then filled with stuffing that is not yet fully cooked. Make sure flour sheets are well sealed. Preheat air fryer to 390° F. Place samosa in air fryer basket and cook for 10 minutes.

Nutritional values per serving: Calories 254; Total Fat 12.2 g; Carbs 9.3 g; Protein 10.2 g

Avocado Fries

Servings: 4

Preparation Time: 10 minutes

Cooking Time: 15 minutes

Ingredients: 1 ounce Aquafina

1 avocado, sliced

½ teaspoon salt

½ cup panko breadcrumbs

Directions: Toss the panko breadcrumbs and salt together in a bowl.
Pour Aquafina into another bowl. Dredge the avocado slices in Aquafina

and then panko breadcrumbs. Arrange the slices in single layer in air fryer basket. Air fry at 390° F for 10 minutes.

Nutritional values per serving: Calories 263; Total Fat 7.4 g; Carbs 6.5 g; Protein 8.2 g

Honey Roasted Carrots

Servings: 2

Preparation Time: 12 minutes

Cooking Time: 15 minutes

Ingredients: 1 tablespoon honey

Salt and pepper to taste

3 cups of baby carrots

1 tablespoon olive oil

Directions: In a mixing bowl, combine carrots, honey, and olive oil. Season with salt and pepper. Cook in air fryer at 390° F for 12 minutes.

Nutritional values per serving: Calories 257; Total Fat 11.6 g; Carbs 8.7 g; Protein 7.3 g

Crispy & Crunchy Baby Corn

Servings: 4

Preparation Time: 10 minutes

Cooking Time: 15 minutes

Ingredients: 1 cup almond flour

1 teaspoon garlic powder

¼ teaspoon chili powder

4 baby corns, boiled

Salt to taste

½ teaspoon carom seeds

Pinch of baking soda

Directions: In a bowl, add flour, chili powder, garlic powder, baking soda, carom seed, and salt. Mix well. Pour a little water into the batter to make a nice batter. Dip boiled baby corn into the batter to coat. Preheat your air fryer to 350° F. Line the air fryer basket with foil and place the baby corns on foil. Cook baby corns for 10 minutes.

Nutritional values per serving: Calories 243; Total Fat 9.6 g; Carbs 8.2 g; Protein 10.3 g

Tasty Tofu

Servings: 4

Preparation Time: 12 minutes

Cooking Time: 15 minutes

Ingredients: ¼ cup cornmeal

15 ounces extra firm tofu, drained, cubed

Salt and pepper to taste

1 teaspoon chili flakes

¾ cup cornstarch

Directions: Line the air fryer basket with aluminum foil and brush with oil. Preheat your air fryer to 370° F. Mix all ingredients in a bowl. Place in air fryer and cook for 12 minutes.

Nutritional values per serving: Calories 246; Total Fat 11.2 g; Carbs 8.7 g; Protein 7.6 g

Crispy Herb Cauliflower Florets

Servings: 2

Preparation Time: 20 minutes

Cooking Time: 15 minutes

Ingredients: 1 egg, beaten

2 tablespoons parmesan cheese, grated

2 cups cauliflower florets, boiled

¼ cup almond flour

1 tablespoon olive oil

Salt to taste

½ tablespoon mixed herbs

½ teaspoon chili powder

½ teaspoon garlic powder

½ cup breadcrumbs

Directions: In a bowl, combine garlic powder, breadcrumbs, chili powder, mixed herbs, salt, and cheese. Add olive oil to the breadcrumb mixture and mix well. Place flour in a bowl and place the egg in another bowl. Dip the cauliflower florets into the beaten egg, then in flour, and coat with breadcrumbs. Preheat your air fryer to 350° F. Place the coated cauliflower florets inside air fryer basket and cook for 20 minutes.

Nutritional values per serving: Calories 253; Total Fat 11.3 g; Carbs 9,5 g; Protein 8.5 g

Roasted Corn

Servings: 8

Preparation Time: 10 minutes

Cooking Time: 15 minutes

Ingredients: 4 ears of corn

Salt and pepper to taste

3 teaspoons vegetable oil

Directions: Remove the husks from corn, wash and pat them dry. Cut if needed to fit into air fryer basket. Drizzle with vegetable oil and season with salt and pepper. Cook at 400° F for 10 minutes.

Nutritional values per serving: Calories 256; Total Fat 9.4 g; Carbs 8.7 g; Protein 9.2 g

Spicy Nuts

Servings: 8

Preparation Time: 4 minutes

Cooking Time: 15 minutes

Ingredients: 2 cups mixed nuts

1 teaspoon chipotle chili powder

1 teaspoon salt

1 teaspoon pepper

1 tablespoon butter, melted

1 teaspoon ground cumin

Directions: In a bowl, add all ingredients and toss to coat. Preheat your air fryer to 350° F for 5 minutes. Add mixed nuts into air fryer basket and roast for 4 minutes.

Nutritional values per serving: Calories 252; Total Fat 8.6 g; Carbs 7.2 g; Protein 8.4 g

Mediterranean Veggie Mix

Servings: 4

Preparation Time: 20 minutes

Cooking Time: 15 minutes

Ingredients: 1 large zucchini, sliced

1 green pepper, sliced

1 large parsnip, peeled and cubed

Salt and black pepper to taste

2 tablespoons honey

2 cloves garlic, crushed

1 teaspoon mixed herbs

1 teaspoon mustard

6 tablespoons olive oil, divided

4 cherry tomatoes

1 medium carrot, peeled and cubed

Directions: Add the zucchini, green pepper, parsnip, cherry tomatoes, carrot to bottom of air fryer. Cover ingredients with 3 tablespoons of oil and adjust the time to 15 minutes. Cook at 360° F. Prepare your marinade by combining remaining ingredients in air fryer safe baking dish. Combine marinade and vegetables in baking dish and stir well. Sprinkle with salt and pepper. Cook it at 390° F for 5 minutes.

Nutritional values per serving: Calories 262; Total Fat 11.3 g; Carbs 9.5g; Protein 7.4 g

Chapter 9: Fish and seafood

Shrimp with Tomatoes & Feta

Servings: 4

Preparation Time: 20 minutes

Cooking Time: 15 minutes

Ingredients: 2 tablespoons butter

1 tablespoon garlic, minced

1 lb. shrimp, peeled and deveined

14 oz. canned crushed tomatoes

1 cup feta cheese, crumbled

Directions: Set the Instant Pot to sauté. Add the butter and wait for it to melt.

Add the garlic and cook until fragrant.

Add the shrimp and tomatoes.

Seal the pot. Set it to manual and cook at low pressure for 1 minute.

Release the pressure quickly. Top with the feta cheese.

Serving Suggestion: Serve with whole wheat toasted bread.

Tip: You can also top with olives.

Nutritional values per serving: Calories 218; Total Fat 10.5 g; Saturated Fat 6.6 g; Cholesterol 192 mg; Sodium 618 mg; Total Carbohydrate 7.9 g; Dietary Fiber 2.2 g; Total Sugars 4.7 g; Protein 22.5 g; Potassium 150 mg

Fish Stew with Tomatoes & Olives

Servings: 4

Preparation Time: 15 minutes

Cooking Time: 25 minutes

Ingredients: 1 1/2 lb. halibut fillet

4 cloves garlic, minced

1 cup cherry tomatoes, sliced in half

3 cups tomato soup

1 cup green olives, pitted and sliced

Directions: Season the fish with salt and pepper.

Pour 1 tablespoon olive oil into the Instant Pot. Add the garlic and cook until fragrant.

Add the fish and cook for 3 minutes per side.

Add the rest of the ingredients.

Cover the pot. Select manual function and cook at low pressure for 3 minutes.

Release the pressure quickly.

Serving Suggestion: Drizzle with olive oil and sprinkle with chopped fresh cilantro.

Tip: You can also sprinkle herbs on both sides of fish fillet.

Nutritional values per serving: Calories 245; Total Fat 3.7 g; Saturated Fat 0.6 g; Cholesterol 35 mg; Sodium 1098 mg; Total Carbohydrate 28 g; Dietary Fiber 2.9 g; Total Sugars 16.5 g; Protein 26.3 g; Potassium 1040 mg

Rosemary Salmon

Servings: 3

Preparation Time: 20 minutes

Cooking Time: 25 minutes

Ingredients: 1 lb. salmon fillets

10 oz. fresh asparagus

1 sprig fresh rosemary

1/2 cup cherry tomatoes, sliced in half

Dressing (mixture of 1 tablespoon olive oil and 1 tablespoon lemon juice)

Directions: Add 1 cup of water into the Instant Pot. Place the steamer rack inside.

Put the salmon fillets on the rack. Add the rosemary and asparagus on top of the salmon.

Cover the pot. Select manual setting and cook at high pressure for 3 minutes.

Release the pressure quickly.

Transfer to a plate. Place the tomatoes on the side.

Drizzle with the dressing.

Serving Suggestion: Garnish with lemon slices.

Nutritional values per serving: Calories 267; Total Fat 14.3 g; Saturated Fat 2.1 g; Cholesterol 67 mg; Sodium 71 mg; Total Carbohydrate 5.2 g; Dietary Fiber 2.5 g; Total Sugars 2.7 g; Protein 31.7 g; Potassium 853 mg

Salmon with Tahini Sauce

Servings: 2

Preparation Time: 10 minutes

Cooking Time: 25 minutes

Ingredients: 1 lb. salmon fillets

3 tablespoons tahini sauce

2 lemon slices

2 sprigs fresh rosemary

Directions: Add the water to the Instant Pot.

Place a steamer basket inside. Put the salmon on top of the basket.

Season with salt and pepper. Place rosemary and lemon slice on top.

Cover the pot. Set it to manual and cook at high pressure for 3 minutes.

Release the pressure quickly.

Drizzle the tahini sauce on top before serving.

Serving Suggestion: Garnish with fresh lemon wedges.

Tip: If you cannot find tahini sauce, you can make your own by mixing the following: 1 tablespoons red wine vinegar, 1 tablespoon lemon juice, 1 clove garlic, minced, ¼ teaspoon dried oregano, Salt and pepper to taste, ¼ cup olive oil, 1 tablespoon crumbled feta cheese.

Nutritional values per serving: Calories 306; Total Fat 14.2 g; Saturated Fat 2.1 g; Cholesterol 100 mg; Sodium 101 mg; Total Carbohydrate 1.4 g; Dietary Fiber 0.7 g; Total Sugars 0.2 g; Protein 44.1 g; Potassium 892 mg

Sautéed Shrimp with Garlic Couscous

Servings: 4

Preparation Time: 10 minutes

Cooking Time: 25 minutes

Ingredients: 1 lb. shrimp, peeled and deveined

1/2 cup fresh chives, chopped

1/2 cup fresh parsley, chopped

1 tablespoon scallions, chopped

10 oz. garlic flavored couscous

Directions: Choose sauté function in the Instant Pot. Add 2 tablespoons of olive oil.

Add the shrimp and herbs, cook for 3 minutes, stirring frequently. Serve with the couscous.

Serving Suggestion: Serve with pasta or rice.

Tip: You can also use plain couscous if you like.

Nutritional values per serving: Calories 615; Total Fat 8.3 g; Saturated Fat 0.6 g; Cholesterol 239 mg; Sodium 1556 mg; Total Carbohydrate 95 g; Dietary Fiber 8 g; Total Sugars 2.7 g; Protein 43.8 g; Potassium 256 mg

Salmon with Garlic & Basil Potatoes

Servings: 4

Preparation Time: 10 minutes

Cooking Time: 25 minutes

Ingredients: 1 lb. baby potatoes

4 tablespoons butter, divided

4 salmon fillets

4 cloves garlic, minced

1 teaspoon dried basil

171

Directions: Put the potatoes in the Instant Pot. Add 1 cup water and half of the butter. Season with salt and pepper.

Put the steamer rack inside the pot, over the potatoes.

Sprinkle both sides of salmon with salt and pepper.

Seal the pot and set it to manual. Cook at high pressure for 3 minutes.

Transfer the salmon to a plate. Remove the potatoes and slice each in half.

Add the remaining butter to the pot. Add the garlic and cook until fragrant.

Put the potatoes back to the pot. Sprinkle with basil leaves and cook for 1 minute.

Serve salmon with potatoes.

Serving Suggestion: Garnish with lemon zest.

Tip: You can also add chopped parsley to the potatoes.

Nutritional values per serving : Calories 408; Total Fat 22.6 g; Saturated Fat 8.9 g; Cholesterol 109 mg; Sodium 172 mg; Total Carbohydrate 15.1 g; Dietary Fiber 2.9 g; Total Sugars 0 g; Protein 37.8 g; Potassium 1168 mg

Chapter 10: Dinner

Chicken Cheese Fillet

Servings: 4

Preparation time: 15 minutes

Cooking Time: 25 minutes

Ingredients: 2 large chicken fillets

4 Gouda cheese slices

4 ham slices

Salt and Pepper to taste

1 tablespoon of chives, chopped

Directions: Preheat your air fryer to 180° F. Cut chicken fillet into four pieces. Make a slit horizontally to the edge. Open the fillet and season with salt and pepper. Cover each piece with chives and cheese slice. Close fillet and wrap in a ham slice. Place wrap chicken fillet into air fryer basket and cook for 15 minutes. Serve hot!

Nutritional values per serving : Calories 386; Total Fat 21 g; Carbs 14.3 g; Protein 30 g

Roasted Pepper Salad

Servings: 4

Preparation time: 10 minutes

Cooking Time: 30 minutes

Ingredients: 1 lettuce cut into broad strips

1 red bell pepper

1 tablespoon lemon juice

3 tablespoons of rocket leaves

Black pepper to taste

2 tablespoons olive oil

3 tablespoons plain yogurt

Directions: Preheat your air fryer to 200° F. Place the bell pepper in air fryer basket and roast for 10 minutes. Add pepper to a bowl, cover with a lid and set aside for 10 minutes. Cut bell pepper into four parts and remove the seeds and skin. Chop the bell pepper into strips. Add lemon juice, yogurt, and oil in a bowl. Season with black pepper. Add lettuce and rocket leaves and toss. Garnish the salad with red bell pepper strips. Serve and enjoy!

Nutritional values per serving: Calories 91; Total Fat 7 g; Carbs 3 g; Protein 2 g

Pineapple Pizza

Servings: 3

Preparation Time: 10 minutes

Cooking Time: 30 minutes

Ingredients: 1 large whole wheat tortilla

¼ cup tomato pizza sauce

¼ cup pineapple tidbits

¼ cup mozzarella cheese, grated

¼ cup ham slice

Directions: Preheat your air fryer to 300° F. Place the tortilla on a baking sheet then spread pizza sauce over tortilla. Arrange ham slice, cheese, pineapple over the tortilla. Place the pizza in the air fryer basket and cook for 10 minutes. Serve hot.

Nutritional values per serving : Calories 80; Total Fat 2 g; Carbs 12 g; Protein 4 g

Air Fryer Tortilla Pizza

Servings: 6

Preparation Time: 7 minutes

Cooking Time: 30 minutes

Ingredients: 1 large whole wheat tortilla

1 tablespoon black olives

Salt and pepper to taste

4 tablespoons tomato sauce

8 pepperoni slices

3 tablespoons of sweet corn

1 medium, tomato, chopped

½ cup mozzarella cheese, grated

Directions: Preheat your air fryer to 325° F. Spread tomato sauce over tortilla. Add pepperoni slices, olives, corn, tomato, and cheese on top of the tortilla. Season with salt and pepper. Place pizza in air fryer basket and cook for 7 minutes. Serve and enjoy!

Nutritional values per serving: Calories 110; Total Fat 5 g; Carbs 10 g; Protein 4 g

Stuffed Garlic Chicken

Servings: 2

Preparation time: 15 minutes

Cooking Time: 30minutes

Ingredients: ¼ cup of tomatoes, sliced

½ tablespoon garlic, minced

2 basil leaves

Salsa for serving

1 prosciutto slice

2 teaspoons parmesan cheese, freshly grated

2 boneless chicken breasts

Pepper and salt to taste

Directions: Cut the side of the chicken breast to make a pocket. Stuff each pocket with tomato slices, garlic, grated cheese and basil leaves. Cut a slice of prosciutto in half to form 2 equal size pieces. Season chicken with salt and pepper and wrap each with a slice of prosciutto. Preheat your air fryer to 325° F. Place the stuffed chicken breasts into air fryer basket and cook for 15 minutes. Serve chicken breasts with salsa.

Rosemary Citrus Chicken

Servings: 2

Preparation Time: 15 minutes

Cooking Time: 30 minutes

Ingredients: 1 lb. chicken thighs

1/2 teaspoon rosemary, fresh, chopped

1/8 teaspoon thyme, dried

½ cup tangerine juice

2 tablespoons white wine

1 teaspoon garlic, minced

Salt and pepper to taste

2 tablespoons lemon juice

Directions: Place the chicken thighs in a mixing bowl. In another bowl, mix tangerine juice, garlic, white wine, lemon juice, rosemary, pepper, salt, and thyme. Pour the mixture over chicken thighs and place in the fridge for 20 minutes. Preheat your air fryer to 350° F and place your marinated chicken in air fryer basket and cook for 15 minutes. Serve hot and enjoy!

Nutritional values per serving: Calories 473; Total Fat 17 g; Carbs 7 g; Protein 66 g

Macaroni Cheese Toast

Servings: 2

Preparation Time: 5 minutes

Cooking Time: 30 minutes

Ingredients: 1 egg, beaten

4 tablespoons cheddar cheese, grated

Salt and pepper to taste

½ cup macaroni and cheese

4 bread slices

Directions: Spread the cheese and macaroni and cheese over the two bread slices. Place the other bread slices on top of cheese and cut diagonally. In a bowl, beat egg and season with salt and pepper. Brush the egg mixture onto the bread. Place the bread into air fryer and cook at 300° F for 5 minutes.

Nutritional values per serving: Calories 250; Total Fat 16 g; Carbs 9 g; Protein 14 g

Cheese Burger Patties

Servings: 6

Preparation Time: 15 minutes

Cooking Time: 30 minutes

Ingredients: 1 lb. ground beef

6 cheddar cheese slices

Pepper and salt to taste

Directions: Preheat your air fryer to 390° F. Season beef with salt and pepper. Make six round shaped patties from the mixture and place them into air fryer basket. Air fry the patties for 10 minutes. Open the air fryer basket and place cheese slices on top of patties and place into air fryer with an additional cook time of 1 minute.

Nutritional Values per serving: Calories 253; Total Fat 14 g; Carbs 0.4 g; Protein 29 g

Grilled Cheese Corn

Servings: 2

Preparation Time: 15 minutes

Cooking Time: 30 minutes

Ingredients: 2 whole corn on the cob, peel husks and discard silk

1 teaspoon olive oil

2 teaspoons paprika

½ cup feta cheese, grated

Directions: Rub the olive oil over corn then sprinkle with paprika and rub all over the corn. Preheat your air fryer to 300° F. Place the seasoned corn on the grill for 15 minutes. Place corn on a serving dish then sprinkle with grated cheese over corn. Serve and enjoy!

Nutritional values per serving : Calories 150; Total Fat 10 g; Carbs 7 g, Protein 7 g

Eggplant Fries

Servings: 4

Preparation time: 20 minutes

Cooking Time: 30minutes

Ingredients: 1 eggplant, cut into 3 inch pieces

¼ cup of water

1 tablespoon of olive oil

4 tablespoons cornstarch

Sea salt to taste

Directions: Preheat your air fryer to 390° F. In a bowl, combine eggplant, water, oil, and cornstarch. Place the eggplant fries in air fryer basket, and air fry them for 20 minutes. Serve warm and enjoy!

Coconut Lime Skirt Steak

Servings: 2

Preparation time: 5 minutes

Cooking Time: 30minutes

Ingredients: ½ cup coconut oil, melted

Zest of one lime

2 1lb. grass fed skirt steaks

¾ teaspoon sea salt

1 teaspoon red pepper flakes

1 teaspoon ginger, fresh, grated

1 tablespoon garlic, minced

2 tablespoons freshly squeezed lime juice

Directions: In a mixing bowl, combine lime juice, coconut oil, garlic, ginger, red pepper, salt, and zest. Add the steaks and toss and rub with marinade. Allow the meat to marinate for about 20 minutes at room temperature. Transfer steaks to your air fryer directly on the rack. Cook steaks in air fryer at 400° F for 5 minutes.

Nutritional values per serving: Calories 312; Total Fat 12.3 g; Carbs 6.4 g; Protein 42.1 g

Chapter 11: Snack and appetizers

Meatballs Platter

Servings: 4

Preparation time: 10 minutes

Cooking time: 15 minutes

Ingredients: 1 pound beef meat, ground

¼ cup panko breadcrumbs

A pinch of salt and black pepper

3 tablespoons red onion, grated

¼ cup parsley, chopped

2 garlic cloves, minced

2 tablespoons lemon juice

Zest of 1 lemon, grated

1 egg

½ teaspoon cumin, ground

½ teaspoon coriander, ground

¼ teaspoon cinnamon powder

2 ounces feta cheese, crumbled

Directions: In a bowl, mix the beef with the breadcrumbs, salt, pepper and the rest of the ingredients except the cooking spray, stir well and shape medium balls out of this mix.

Arrange the meatballs on a baking sheet lined with parchment paper, grease them with cooking spray and bake at 450°F for 15 minutes.

Arrange the meatballs on a platter and serve as an appetizer.

Nutritional values per serving: Calories 300; Fat 15.4 g; Fiber 6.4 g, Carbs 22.4 g; Protein 35 g

Yogurt Dip

Servings: 6

Preparation time: 10 minutes

Cooking time: 0 minutes

Ingredients: 2 cups Greek yogurt

2 tablespoons pistachios, toasted and chopped

A pinch of salt and white pepper

2 tablespoons mint, chopped

1 tablespoon kalamata olives, pitted and chopped

¼ cup za'atar spice

¼ cup pomegranate seeds

1/3 cup olive oil

Directions: In a bowl, combine the yogurt with the pistachios and the rest of the ingredients, whisk well, divide into small cups and serve with pita chips on the side.

Nutritional values per serving: Calories 294; Fat 18 g; Fiber 1 g; Carbs 21 g; Protein 10 g

Tomato Bruschetta

Servings: 6

Preparation time: 10 minutes

Cooking time: 10 minutes

Ingredients: 1 baguette, sliced

1/3 cup basil, chopped

6 tomatoes, cubed

2 garlic cloves, minced

A pinch of salt and black pepper

1 teaspoon olive oil

1 tablespoon balsamic vinegar

½ teaspoon garlic powder

Cooking spray

Directions: Arrange the baguette slices on a baking sheet lined with parchment paper, grease them with cooking spray and bake at 400° F for 10 minutes.

In a bowl, mix the tomatoes with the basil and the remaining ingredients, toss well and leave aside for 10 minutes.

Divide the tomato mix on each baguette slice, arrange them all on a platter and serve.

Nutritional values per serving: Calories 162; Fat 4 g; Fiber 7 g; Carbs 29 g; Protein 4 g

Artichoke Flatbread

Servings: 4

Preparation time: 10 minutes

Cooking time: 15 minutes

Ingredients: 5 tablespoons olive oil

2 garlic cloves, minced

2 tablespoons parsley, chopped

2 round whole wheat flatbreads

4 tablespoons parmesan, grated

½ cup mozzarella cheese, grated

14 ounces canned artichokes, drained and quartered

1 cup baby spinach, chopped

½ cup cherry tomatoes, halved

½ teaspoon basil, dried

Salt and black pepper to the taste

Directions: In a bowl, mix the parsley with the garlic and 4 tablespoons oil, whisk well and spread this over the flatbreads.

Sprinkle the mozzarella and half of the parmesan.

In a bowl, mix the artichokes with the spinach, tomatoes, basil, salt, pepper and the rest of the oil, toss and divide over the flatbreads as well.

Sprinkle the rest of the parmesan on top, arrange the flatbreads on a baking sheet lined with parchment paper and bake at 425° F for 15 minutes.

Serve as an appetizer.

Nutritional values per serving: Calories 223; Fat 11.2 g; Fiber 5.34 g, Carbs 15.5 g; Protein 7.4 g

Red Pepper Tapenade

Servings: 4

Preparation time: 10 minutes

Cooking time: 0 minutes

Ingredients: 7 ounces roasted red peppers, chopped

½ cup parmesan, grated

1/3 cup parsley, chopped

14 ounces canned artichokes, drained and chopped

3 tablespoons olive oil

¼ cup capers, drained

1 and ½ tablespoons lemon juice

2 garlic cloves, minced

Directions: In your blender, combine the red peppers with the parmesan and the rest of the ingredients and pulse well.

Divide into cups and serve as a snack.

Nutritional values per serving: Calories 200; Fat 5.6 g; Fiber 4.5 g; Carbs 12.4 g; Protein 4.6 g

Coriander Falafel

Servings: 8

Preparation time: 10 minutes

Cooking time: 10 minutes

Ingredients: 1 cup canned garbanzo beans, drained and rinsed

1 bunch parsley leaves

1 yellow onion, chopped

5 garlic cloves, minced

1 teaspoon coriander, ground

A pinch of salt and black pepper

¼ teaspoon cayenne pepper

¼ teaspoon baking soda

¼ teaspoon cumin powder

1 teaspoon lemon juice

3 tablespoons tapioca flour

Olive oil for frying

Directions: In your food processor, combine the beans with the parsley, onion and the rest the ingredients except the oil and the flour and pulse well.

Transfer the mix to a bowl, add the flour, stir well, shape 16 balls out of this mix and flatten them a bit.

Heat up a pan with some oil over medium-high heat, add the falafels, cook them for 5 minutes on each side, transfer to paper towels, drain excess grease, arrange them on a platter and serve as an appetizer.

Nutritional values per serving: Calories 112; Fat 6.2 g; Fiber 2 g; Carbs 12.3 g; Protein 3.1g

Red Pepper Hummus

Servings: 6

Preparation time: 10 minutes

Cooking time: 0 minutes

Ingredients: 6 ounces roasted red peppers, peeled and chopped

16 ounces canned chickpeas, drained and rinsed

¼ cup Greek yogurt

3 tablespoons tahini paste

Juice of 1 lemon

3 garlic cloves, minced

1 tablespoon olive oil

A pinch of salt and black pepper

1 tablespoon parsley, chopped

Directions: In your food processor, combine the red peppers with the rest of the ingredients except the oil and the parsley and pulse well.

Add the oil, pulse again, divide into cups, sprinkle the parsley on top and serve as a party spread.

Nutritional values per serving: Calories 255; Fat 11.4 g; Fiber 4.5 g; Carbs 17.4 g; Protein 6.5 g

White Bean Dip

Servings: 4

Preparation time: 10 minutes

Cooking time: 0 minute

Ingredients: 15 ounces canned white beans, drained and rinsed

6 ounces canned artichoke hearts, drained and quartered

4 garlic cloves, minced

1 tablespoon basil, chopped

2 tablespoons olive oil

Juice of ½ lemon

Zest of ½ lemon, grated

Salt and black pepper to the taste

Directions: In your food processor, combine the beans with the artichokes and the rest of the ingredients except the oil and pulse well.

Add the oil gradually, pulse the mix again, divide into cups and serve as a party dip.

Nutritional values per serving: Calories 274; Fat 11.7 g; Fiber 6.5 g; Carbs 18.5 g; Protein 16.5 g

Hummus with Ground Lamb

Servings: 8

Preparation time: 10 minutes

Cooking time: 15 minute

Ingredients: 10 ounces hummus

12 ounces lamb meat, ground

½ cup pomegranate seeds

¼ cup parsley, chopped

1 tablespoon olive oil

Pita chips for serving

Directions: Heat up a pan with the oil over medium-high heat, add the meat, and brown for 15 minutes stirring often.

Spread the hummus on a platter, spread the ground lamb all over, also spread the pomegranate seeds and the parsley and serve with pita chips as a snack.

Nutritional values per serving: Calories 133; Fat 9.7 g; Fiber 1.7 g; Carbs 6.4 g; Protein 5

Eggplant Dip

Servings: 4

Preparation time: 10 minutes

Cooking time: 40 minutes

Ingredients: 1 eggplant, poked with a fork

2 tablespoons tahini paste

2 tablespoons lemon juice

2 garlic cloves, minced

1 tablespoon olive oil

Salt and black pepper to the taste

1 tablespoon parsley, chopped

Directions: Put the eggplant in a roasting pan, bake at 400° F for 40 minutes, cool down, peel and transfer to your food processor.

Add the rest of the ingredients except the parsley, pulse well, divide into small bowls and serve as an appetizer with the parsley sprinkled on top.

Nutritional values per serving: Calories 121; Fat 4.3 g; Fiber 1 g; Carbs 1.4 g; Protein 4.3 g

Veggie Fritters

Servings: 8

Preparation time: 10 minutes

Cooking time: 10 minutes

Ingredients: 2 garlic cloves, minced

2 yellow onions, chopped

4 scallions, chopped

2 carrots, grated

2 teaspoons cumin, ground

½ teaspoon turmeric powder

Salt and black pepper to the taste

¼ teaspoon coriander, ground

2 tablespoons parsley, chopped

¼ teaspoon lemon juice

½ cup almond flour

2 beets, peeled and grated

2 eggs, whisked

¼ cup tapioca flour

3 tablespoons olive oil

Directions: In a bowl, combine the garlic with the onions, scallions and the rest of the ingredients except the oil, stir well and shape medium fritters out of this mix.

Heat up a pan with the oil over medium-high heat, add the fritters, cook for 5 minutes on each side, arrange on a platter and serve.

Nutritional values per serving: Calories 209; Fat 11.2 g; Fiber 3 g; Carbs 4.4 g; Protein 4.8 g

Bulgur Lamb Meatballs

Servings: 6

Preparation time: 10 minutes

Cooking time: 15 minute

Ingredients: 1 and ½ cups Greek yogurt

½ teaspoon cumin, ground

1 cup cucumber, shredded

½ teaspoon garlic, minced

A pinch of salt and black pepper

1 cup bulgur

2 cups water

1 pound lamb, ground

¼ cup parsley, chopped

¼ cup shallots, chopped

½ teaspoon allspice, ground

½ teaspoon cinnamon powder

1 tablespoon olive oil

Directions: In a bowl, combine the bulgur with the water, cover the bowl, leave aside for 10 minutes, drain and transfer to a bowl.

Add the meat, the yogurt and the rest of the ingredients except the oil, stir well and shape medium meatballs out of this mix.

Heat up a pan with the oil over medium-high heat, add the meatballs, cook them for 7 minutes on each side, arrange them all on a platter and serve as an appetizer.

Nutritional values per serving: Calories 300; Fat 9.6 g; Fiber 4.6 g; Carbs 22.6 g; Protein 6.6 g

Cucumber Bites

Servings: 12

Preparation time: 10 minutes

Cooking time: 0 minutes

Ingredients: 1 English cucumber, sliced into 32 rounds

10 ounces hummus

16 cherry tomatoes, halved

1 tablespoon parsley, chopped

1 ounce feta cheese, crumbled

Directions: Spread the hummus on each cucumber round, divide the tomato halves on each, sprinkle the cheese and parsley on to and serve as an appetizer.

Nutritional values per serving: Calories 162; Fat 3.4 g; Fiber 2 g; Carbs 6.4 g; Protein 2.4 g

Stuffed Avocado

Servings: 2

Preparation time: 10 minutes

Cooking time: 0 minute

Ingredients: 1 avocado, halved and pitted

10 ounces canned tuna, drained

2 tablespoons sun-dried tomatoes, chopped

1 and ½ tablespoon basil pesto

2 tablespoons black olives, pitted and chopped

Salt and black pepper to the taste

2 teaspoons pine nuts, toasted and chopped

1 tablespoon basil, chopped

Directions: In a bowl, combine the tuna with the sun-dried tomatoes and the rest of the ingredients except the avocado and stir.

Stuff the avocado halves with the tuna mix and serve as an appetizer.

Nutritional values per serving: Calories 233; Fat 9 g; Fiber 3.5 g; Carbs 11.4 g; Protein 5.6 g

Wrapped Plums

Servings: 8

Preparation time: 5 minutes

Cooking time: 0 minutes

Ingredients: 2 ounces prosciutto, cut into 16 pieces

4 plums, quartered

1 tablespoon chives, chopped

A pinch of red pepper flakes, crushed

Directions: Wrap each plum quarter in a prosciutto slice, arrange them all on a platter, sprinkle the chives and pepper flakes all over and serve.

Nutritional values per serving: Calories 30; Fat 1 g; Fiber 0 g; Carbs 4 g; Protein 2 g

Cucumber Sandwich Bites

Servings: 12

Preparation time: 5 minutes

Cooking time: 0 minutes

Ingredients: 1 cucumber, sliced

8 slices whole wheat bread

2 tablespoons cream cheese, soft

1 tablespoon chives, chopped

¼ cup avocado, peeled, pitted and mashed

1 teaspoon mustard

Salt and black pepper to the taste

Directions: Spread the mashed avocado on each bread slice, also spread the rest of the ingredients except the cucumber slices. Divide the cucumber slices on the bread slices, cut each slice in thirds, arrange on a platter and serve as an appetizer.

Nutritional values per serving: Calories 187; Fat 12.4 g; Fiber 2.1 g; Carbs 4.5 g; Protein 8.2 g

Cucumber Rolls

Servings: 6

Preparation time: 5 minutes

Cooking time: 0 minutes

Ingredients: 1 big cucumber, sliced lengthwise

1 tablespoon parsley, chopped

8 ounces canned tuna, drained and mashed

Salt and black pepper to the taste

1 teaspoon lime juice

Directions: Arrange cucumber slices on a working surface, divide the rest of the ingredients, and roll.

Arrange all the rolls on a platter and serve as an appetizer.

Nutritional values per serving: Calories 200; Fat 6 g; Fiber 3.4 g; Carbs 7.6 g; Protein 3.5 g

Olives and Cheese Stuffed Tomatoes

Servings: 24

Preparation time: 10 minutes

Cooking time: 0 minutes

Ingredients: 24 cherry tomatoes, top cut off and insides scooped out

2 tablespoons olive oil

¼ teaspoon red pepper flakes

½ cup feta cheese, crumbled

2 tablespoons black olive paste

¼ cup mint, torn

Directions: In a bowl, mix the olives paste with the rest of the ingredients except the cherry tomatoes and whisk well. Stuff the cherry tomatoes with this mix, arrange them all on a platter and serve as an appetizer.

Nutritional values per serving: Calories 136; Fat 8.6 g; Fiber 4.8 g; Carbs 5.6 g; Protein 5.1 g

Tomato Salsa

Servings: 6

Preparation time: 5 minutes

Cooking time: 0 minutes

Ingredients: 1 garlic clove, minced

4 tablespoons olive oil

5 tomatoes, cubed

1 tablespoon balsamic vinegar

¼ cup basil, chopped

1 tablespoon parsley, chopped

1 tablespoon chives, chopped

Salt and black pepper to the taste

Pita chips for serving

Directions: In a bowl, mix the tomatoes with the garlic and the rest of the ingredients except the pita chips, stir, divide into small cups and serve with the pita chips on the side.

Nutritional values per serving: Calories 160; Fat 13.7 g; Fiber 5.5 g; Carbs 10.1 g; Protein 2.2

Chili Mango and Watermelon Salsa

Servings: 12

Preparation time: 5 minutes

Cooking time: 0 minutes

Ingredients: 1 red tomato, chopped

Salt and black pepper to the taste

1 cup watermelon, seedless, peeled and cubed

1 red onion, chopped

2 mangos, peeled and chopped

2 chili peppers, chopped

¼ cup cilantro, chopped

3 tablespoons lime juice

Pita chips for serving

Directions: In a bowl, mix the tomato with the watermelon, the onion and the rest of the ingredients except the pita chips and toss well. Divide the mix into small cups and serve with pita chips on the side.

Nutritional values per serving: Calories 62; Fat 4.7 g; Fiber 1.3 g; Carbs 3.9 g; Protein 2.3 g

Creamy Spinach and Shallots Dip

Servings: 4

Preparation time: 10 minutes

Cooking time: 0 minutes

Ingredients: 1 pound spinach, roughly chopped

2 shallots, chopped

2 tablespoons mint, chopped

¾ cup cream cheese, soft

Salt and black pepper to the taste

Directions: In a blender, combine the spinach with the shallots and the rest of the ingredients, and pulse well. Divide into small bowls and serve as a party dip.

Nutritional values per serving: Calories 204; Fat 11.5 g; Fiber 3.1 g; Carbs 4.2 g; Protein 5.9 g

Feta Artichoke Dip

Servings: 8

Preparation time: 10 minutes

Cooking time: 30 minutes

Ingredients: 8 ounces artichoke hearts, drained and quartered

¾ cup basil, chopped

¾ cup green olives, pitted and chopped

1 cup parmesan cheese, grated

5 ounces feta cheese, crumbled

Directions: In your food processor, mix the artichokes with the basil and the rest of the ingredients, pulse well, and transfer to a baking dish.

Introduce in the oven, bake at 375° F for 30 minutes and serve as a party dip.

Nutritional values per serving: Calories 186; Fat 12.4 g; Fiber 0.9 g; Carbs 2.6 g; Protein 1.5 g

Avocado Dip

Servings: 8

Preparation time: 5 minutes

Cooking time: 0 minutes

Ingredients: ½ cup heavy cream

1 green chili pepper, chopped

Salt and pepper to the taste

4 avocados, pitted, peeled and chopped

1 cup cilantro, chopped

¼ cup lime juice

Directions: In a blender, combine the cream with the avocados and the rest of the ingredients and pulse well. Divide the mix into bowls and serve cold as a party dip.

Nutritional values per serving: Calories 200; Fat 14.5 g; Fiber 3.8 g; Carbs 8.1 g; Protein 7.6 g

Goat Cheese and Chives Spread

Servings: 4

Preparation time: 10 minutes

Cooking time: 0 minutes

Ingredients: 2 ounces goat cheese, crumbled

¾ cup sour cream

2 tablespoons chives, chopped

1 tablespoon lemon juice

Salt and black pepper to the taste

2 tablespoons extra virgin olive oil

Directions: In a bowl, mix the goat cheese with the cream and the rest of the ingredients and whisk really well. Keep in the fridge for 10 minutes and serve as a party spread.

Nutritional values per serving: Calories 220; Fat 11.5 g; Fiber 4.8 g; Carbs 8.9 g; Protein 5.6 g

Ginger and Cream Cheese Dip

Servings: 6

Preparation time: 5 minutes

Cooking time: 0 minutes

Ingredients: ½ cup ginger, grated

2 bunches cilantro, chopped

3 tablespoons balsamic vinegar

½ cup olive oil

1 and ½ cups cream cheese, soft

Directions: In your blender, mix the ginger with the rest of the ingredients and pulse well.

Divide into small bowls and serve as a party dip.

Nutritional values per serving: Calories 213; Fat 4.9 g; Fiber 4.1 g; Carbs 8.8 g; Protein 17.8 g

Walnuts Yogurt Dip

Servings: 8

Preparation time: 5 minutes

Cooking time: 0 minutes

Ingredients: 3 garlic cloves, minced

2 cups Greek yogurt

¼ cup dill, chopped

1 tablespoon chives, chopped

¼ cup walnuts, chopped

Salt and black pepper to the taste

Directions: In a bowl, mix the garlic with the yogurt and the rest of the ingredients, whisk well, divide into small cups and serve as a party dip.

Nutritional values per serving: Calories 200; Fat 6.5 g; Fiber 4.6 g; Carbs 15.5 g; Protein 8.4 g

Herbed Goat Cheese Dip

Servings: 4

Preparation time: 5 minutes

Cooking time: 0 minutes

Ingredients: ¼ cup mixed parsley, chopped

¼ cup chives, chopped

8 ounces goat cheese, soft

Salt and black pepper to the taste

A drizzle of olive oil

Directions: In your food processor mix the goat cheese with the parsley and the rest of the ingredients and pulse well.

Divide into small bowls and serve as a party dip.

Nutritional values per serving: Calories 245; Fat 11.3 g; Fiber 4.5 g; Carbs 8.9 g; Protein 11.2 g

Scallions Dip

Servings: 8

Preparation time: 5 minutes

Cooking time: 0 minutes

Ingredients: 6 scallions, chopped

1 garlic clove, minced

3 tablespoons olive oil

Salt and black pepper to the taste

1 tablespoon lemon juice

1 and ½ cups cream cheese, soft

2 ounces prosciutto, cooked and crumbled

Directions: In a bowl, mix the scallions with the garlic and the rest of the ingredients except the prosciutto and whisk well.

Divide into bowls, sprinkle the prosciutto on top and serve as a party dip.

Nutritional values per serving: Calories 144; Fat 7.7 g; Fiber 1.4 g; Carbs 6.3 g; Protein 5.5 g

Tomato Cream Cheese Spread

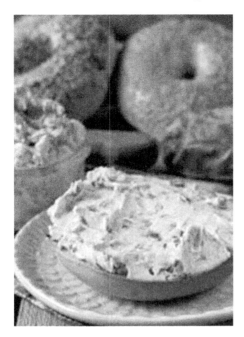

Servings: 6

Preparation time: 5 minutes

Cooking time: 0 minutes

Ingredients: 12 ounces cream cheese, soft

1 big tomato, cubed

¼ cup homemade mayonnaise

2 garlic clove, minced

2 tablespoons red onion, chopped

2 tablespoons lime juice

Salt and black pepper to the taste

Directions: In your blender, mix the cream cheese with the tomato and the rest of the ingredients, pulse well, divide into small cups and serve cold.

Nutritional values per serving: Calories 204; Fat 6.7 g; Fiber 1.4 g; Carbs 7.3 g; Protein 4.5 g

Pesto Dip

Servings: 6

Preparation time: 5 minutes

Cooking time: 0 minutes

Ingredients: 1 cup cream cheese, soft

3 tablespoons basil pesto

Salt and black pepper to the taste

1 cup heavy cream

1 tablespoon chives, chopped

Directions: In a bowl, mix the cream cheese with the pesto and the rest of the ingredients and whisk well. Divide into small cups and serve as a party dip.

Nutritional values per serving: Calories 230; Fat 14.5 g; Fiber 4.8 g; Carbs 6.5 g; Protein 5.4 g

Vinegar Beet Bites

Servings: 4

Preparation time: 10 minutes

Cooking time: 30 minutes

Ingredients: 2 beets, sliced

A pinch of sea salt and black pepper

1/3 cup balsamic vinegar

1 cup olive oil

Directions: Spread the beet slices on a baking sheet lined with parchment paper, add the rest of the ingredients, toss and bake at 350° F for 30 minutes. Serve the beet bites cold as a snack.

Nutritional values per serving: Calories 199; Fat 5.4 g; Fiber 3.5 g; Carbs 8.5 g; Protein 3.5 g

Zucchini and Olives Salsa

Servings: 4

Preparation time: 5 minutes

Cooking time: 0 minutes

Ingredients: ½ cup black olives, pitted and sliced

3 zucchinis, cut with a spiralizer

1 cup cherry tomatoes, halved

Salt and black pepper to the taste

1 small red onion, chopped

½ cup feta cheese, crumbled

½ cup olive oil

¼ cup apple cider vinegar

Directions: In a bowl, mix the olives with the zucchinis and the rest of the ingredients, toss, divide into small cups and serve as an appetizer.

Nutritional values per serving: Calories 140; Fat 14.2 g; Fiber 1.4 g; Carbs 3.5 g; Protein 1.4 g

Strawberry and Carrots Salad

Servings: 4

Preparation time: 5 minutes

Cooking time: 0 minute

Ingredients: 6 carrots, peeled and grated

10 strawberries, halved

Salt and black pepper to the taste

2 tablespoons balsamic vinegar

1 tablespoon Dijon mustard

¼ cup lemon juice

2 tablespoons olive oil

Directions: In a bowl, mix the carrots with the strawberries and the rest of the ingredients, toss, divide between appetizer plates and serve.

Nutritional values per serving: Calories 182; Fat 4.3 g; Fiber 2.4 g; Carbs 7.5 g; Protein 3 g

Hot Squash Wedges

Servings: 6

Preparation time: 10 minutes

Cooking time: 25 minutes

Ingredients: 6 tablespoons olive oil

2 tablespoons chili paste

3 butternut squash, peeled and cut into wedges

2 tablespoons balsamic vinegar

1 tablespoon chives, chopped

Directions: In a bowl, mix the squash wedges with the chili paste and the rest of the ingredients, toss, spread them on a baking sheet lined with parchment paper and bake at 400° F for 25 minutes, flipping them from time to time. Divide the wedges into bowls and serve as a snack.

Nutritional values per serving: Calories 180; Fat 4.2 g; Fiber 4.4 g; Carbs 6.5 g; Protein 1.4 g

Shrimp and Cucumber Bites

Servings: 8

Preparation time: 5 minutes

Cooking time: 0 minutes

Ingredients: 1 big cucumber, cubed

1 pound shrimp, cooked, peeled, deveined and chopped

2 tablespoons heavy cream

Salt and black pepper to the taste

12 whole grain crackers

Directions: In a bowl, mix the cucumber with the rest of the ingredients except the crackers and stir well.

Arrange the crackers on a platter, spread the shrimp mix on each and serve.

Nutritional values per serving: Calories 155; Fat 8.5 g; Fiber 4.8 g; Carbs 11.8 g; Protein 17.7 g

Salmon Rolls

Servings: 12

Preparation time: 5 minutes

Cooking time: 0 minutes

Ingredients: 1 big long cucumber, thinly sliced lengthwise

2 teaspoons lime juice

4 ounces cream cheese, soft

1 teaspoon lemon zest, grated

Salt and black pepper to the taste

2 teaspoons dill, chopped

4 ounces smoked salmon, cut into strips

Directions: Arrange cucumber slices on a working surface and top each with a salmon strip.

In a bowl, mix the rest of the ingredients, stir and spread over the salmon.

Roll the salmon and cucumber strips, arrange them on a platter and serve as an appetizer.

Nutritional values per serving: Calories 245; Fat 15.5 g; Fiber 4.8 g; Carbs 16.8 g; Protein 17.3 g

Eggplant Bombs

Servings: 6

Preparation time: 10 minutes

Cooking time: 45 minutes

Ingredients: 4 cups eggplants, chopped

3 tablespoons olive oil

3 garlic cloves, minced

2 eggs, whisked

Salt and black pepper to the taste

1 cup parsley, chopped

½ cup parmesan cheese, finely grated

¾ cups bread crumbs

Directions: Heat up a pan with the oil over medium high heat, add the garlic and the eggplants, and cook for 15 minutes stirring often.

In a bowl, combine the eggplant mix with the rest of the ingredients, stir well and shape medium balls out of this mix.

Arrange the balls on a baking sheet lined with parchment paper and bake at 350° F for 30 minutes.

Serve as a snack.

Nutritional values per serving: Calories 224; Fat 10.6 g; Fiber 1.8 g; Carbs 5.4 g; Protein 3.5

Eggplant Bites

Servings: 8

Preparation time: 10 minutes

Cooking time: 15 minutes

Ingredients: 2 eggplants, cut into 20 slices

2 tablespoons olive oil

½ cup roasted peppers, chopped

½ cup kalamata olives, pitted and chopped

1 tablespoon lime juice

1 teaspoon red pepper flakes, crushed

Salt and black pepper to the taste

2 tablespoons mint, chopped

Directions: In a bowl, mix the roasted peppers with the olives, half of the oil and the rest of the ingredients except the eggplant slices and stir well. Brush eggplant slices with the rest of the olive oil on both sides, place them on the preheated grill over medium high heat, cook for 7 minutes on each side and transfer them to a platter.

Top each eggplant slice with roasted peppers mix and serve.

Nutritional values per serving: Calories 214; Fat 10.6 g; Fiber 5.8 g; Carbs 15.4 g; Protein 5.4 g

Chapter 12: Desserts

Cold Lemon Squares

Servings: 4

Preparation time: 30 minutes

Cooking time: 0 minutes

Ingredients: 1 cup avocado oil + a drizzle

2 bananas, peeled and chopped

1 tablespoon honey

¼ cup lemon juice

A pinch of lemon zest, grated

Directions: In your food processor, mix the bananas with the rest of the ingredients, pulse well and spread on the bottom of a pan greased with a drizzle of oil. Put in the fridge for 30 minutes, slice into squares and serve.

Nutritional values per serving: Calories 136; Fat 11.2 g; Fiber 0.2 g; Carbs 7 g; Protein 1.1 g

Blackberry and Apples Cobbler

Servings: 6

Preparation time: 10 minutes

Cooking time: 30 minutes

Ingredients: ¾ cup stevia

6 cups blackberries

¼ cup apples, cored and cubed

¼ teaspoon baking powder

1 tablespoon lime juice

½ cup almond flour

½ cup water

3 and ½ tablespoon avocado oil

Cooking spray

Directions: In a bowl, mix the berries with half of the stevia and lemon juice, sprinkle some flour all over, whisk and pour into a baking dish greased with cooking spray. In another bowl, mix flour with the rest of the sugar, baking powder, the water and the oil, and stir the whole thing with your hands. Spread over the berries, introduce in the oven at 375° F and bake for 30 minutes. Serve warm.

Nutritional values per serving: Calories 221; Fat 6.3 g; Fiber 3.3 g; Carbs 6 g; Protein 9 g

Black Tea Cake

Servings: 8

Preparation time: 10 minutes

Cooking time: 35 minutes

Ingredients: 6 tablespoons black tea powder

2 cups almond milk, warmed up

1 cup avocado oil

2 cups stevia

4 eggs

2 teaspoons vanilla extract

3 and ½ cups almond flour

1 teaspoon baking soda

3 teaspoons baking powder

Directions: In a bowl, combine the almond milk with the oil, stevia and the rest of the ingredients and whisk well.

Pour this into a cake pan lined with parchment paper, introduce in the oven at 350° F and bake for 35 minutes.

Leave the cake to cool down, slice and serve.

Nutritional values per serving: Calories 200; Fat 6.4 g; Fiber 4 g; Carbs 6.5 g; Protein 5.4 g

Green Tea and Vanilla Cream

Servings: 4

Preparation time: 2 hours

Cooking time: 0 minutes

Ingredients: 14 ounces almond milk, hot

2 tablespoons green tea powder

14 ounces heavy cream

3 tablespoons stevia

1 teaspoon vanilla extract

1 teaspoon gelatin powder

Directions: In a bowl, combine the almond milk with the green tea powder and the rest of the ingredients, whisk well, cool down, divide into cups and keep in the fridge for 2 hours before serving.

Nutritional values per serving: Calories 120; Fat 3 g; Fiber 3 g; Carbs 7 g; Protein 4 g

Figs Pie

Servings: 8

Preparation time: 10 minutes

Cooking time: 1 hour

Ingredients: ½ cup stevia

6 figs, cut into quarters

½ teaspoon vanilla extract

1 cup almond flour

4 eggs, whisked

Directions: Spread the figs on the bottom of a spring form pan lined with parchment paper.

In a bowl, combine the other ingredients, whisk and pour over the figs,

Bake at 375° F for 1 hour, flip the pie upside down when it's done and serve.

Nutritional values per serving: Calories 200; Fat 4.4 g; Fiber 3 g; Carbs 7.6 g; Protein 8 g

Cherry Cream

Servings: 4

Preparation time: 2 hours

Cooking time: 0 minutes

Ingredients: 2 cups cherries, pitted and chopped

1 cup almond milk

½ cup whipping cream

3 eggs, whisked

1/3 cup stevia

1 teaspoon lemon juice

½ teaspoon vanilla extract

Directions: In your food processor, combine the cherries with the milk and the rest of the ingredients, pulse well, divide into cups and keep in the fridge for 2 hours before serving.

Nutritional values per serving: Calories 200; Fat 4.5 g; Fiber 3.3 g; Carbs 5.6 g; Protein 3.4 g

Strawberries Cream

Servings: 4

Preparation time: 10 minutes

Cooking time: 20 minutes

Ingredients: ½ cup stevia

2 pounds strawberries, chopped

1 cup almond milk

Zest of 1 lemon, grated

½ cup heavy cream

3 egg yolks, whisked

Directions: Heat up a pan with the milk over medium-high heat, add the stevia and the rest of the ingredients, whisk well, simmer for 20 minutes, divide into cups and serve cold.

Nutritional values per serving: Calories 152; Fat 4.4 g; Fiber 5.5 g; Carbs 5.1 g; Protein 0.8 g

Apples and Plum Cake

Servings: 4

Preparation time: 10 minutes

Cooking time: 40 minutes

Ingredients: 7 ounces almond flour

1 egg, whisked

5 tablespoons stevia

3 ounces warm almond milk

2 pounds plums, pitted and cut into quarters

2 apples, cored and chopped

Zest of 1 lemon, grated

1 teaspoon baking powder

Directions: In a bowl, mix the almond milk with the egg, stevia, and the rest of the ingredients except the cooking spray and whisk well.

Grease a cake pan with the oil, pour the cake mix inside, introduce in the oven and bake at 350° F for 40 minutes.

Cool down, slice and serve.

Nutritional values per serving: Calories 209; Fat 6.4 g; Fiber 6 g; Carbs 8 g; Protein 6.6 g

Cinnamon Chickpeas Cookies

Servings: 12

Preparation time: 10 minutes

Cooking time: 20 minutes

Ingredients: 1 cup canned chickpeas, drained, rinsed and mashed

2 cups almond flour

1 teaspoon cinnamon powder

1 teaspoon baking powder

1 cup avocado oil

½ cup stevia

1 egg, whisked

2 teaspoons almond extract

1 cup raisins

1 cup coconut, unsweetened and shredded

Directions: In a bowl, combine the chickpeas with the flour, cinnamon and the other ingredients, and whisk well until you obtain a dough.

Scoop tablespoons of dough on a baking sheet lined with parchment paper, introduce them in the oven at 350° F and bake for 20 minutes.

Leave them to cool down for a few minutes and serve.

Nutritional values per serving: Calories 200; Fat 4.5 g; Fiber 3.4 g; Carbs 9.5 g; Protein 2.4 g

Cocoa Brownies

Servings: 8

Preparation time: 10 minutes

Cooking time: 20 minutes

Ingredients: 30 ounces canned lentils, rinsed and drained

1 tablespoon honey

1 banana, peeled and chopped

½ teaspoon baking soda

4 tablespoons almond butter

2 tablespoons cocoa powder

Cooking spray

Directions: In a food processor, combine the lentils with the honey and the other ingredients except the cooking spray and pulse well.

Pour this into a pan greased with cooking spray, spread evenly, introduce in the oven at 375° F and bake for 20 minutes.

Cut the brownies and serve cold.

Nutritional values per serving: Calories 200; Fat 4.5 g; Fiber 2.4 g; Carbs 8.7 g; Protein 4.3 g

Cardamom Almond Cream

Servings: 4

Preparation time: 30 minutes

Cooking time: 0 minutes

Ingredients: Juice of 1 lime

½ cup stevia

1 and ½ cups water

3 cups almond milk

½ cup honey

2 teaspoons cardamom, ground

1 teaspoon rose water

1 teaspoon vanilla extract

Directions: In a blender, combine the almond milk with the cardamom and the rest of the ingredients, pulse well, divide into cups and keep in the fridge for 30 minutes before serving.

Nutritional values per serving: Calories 283; Fat 11.8 g; Fiber 0.3 g; Carbs 4.7 g; Protein 7.1 g

Banana Cinnamon Cupcakes

Servings: 4

Preparation time: 10 minutes

Cooking time: 20 minutes

Ingredients: 4 tablespoons avocado oil

4 eggs

½ cup orange juice

2 teaspoons cinnamon powder

1 teaspoon vanilla extract

2 bananas, peeled and chopped

¾ cup almond flour

½ teaspoon baking powder

Cooking spray

Directions: In a bowl, combine the oil with the eggs, orange juice and the other ingredients except the cooking spray, whisk well, pour in a cupcake pan greased with the cooking spray, introduce in the oven at 350° F and bake for 20 minutes. Cool the cupcakes down and serve.

Nutritional values per serving: Calories 142; Fat 5.8 g; Fiber 4.2 g; Carbs 5.7 g; Protein 1.6 g

Rhubarb and Apples Cream

Servings: 6

Preparation time: 10 minutes

Cooking time: 0 minutes

Ingredients: 3 cups rhubarb, chopped

1 and ½ cups stevia

2 eggs, whisked

½ teaspoon nutmeg, ground

1 tablespoon avocado oil

1/3 cup almond milk

Directions: In a blender, combine the rhubarb with the stevia and the rest of the ingredients, pulse well, divide into cups and serve cold.

Nutritional values per serving: Calories 200; Fat 5.2 g; Fiber 3.4 g; Carbs 7.6 g; Protein 2.5 g

Almond Rice Dessert

Servings: 4

Preparation time: 10 minute

Cooking time: 20 minutes

Ingredients: 1 cup white rice

2 cups almond milk

1 cup almonds, chopped

½ cup stevia

1 tablespoon cinnamon powder

½ cup pomegranate seeds

Directions: In a pot, mix the rice with the milk and stevia, bring to a simmer and cook for 20 minutes, stirring often.

Add the rest of the ingredients, stir, divide into bowls and serve.

Nutritional values per serving: Calories 234; Fat 9.5 g; Fiber 3.4 g; Carbs 12.4 g; Protein 6.5 g

Peach Sorbet

Servings: 4

Preparation time: 2 hours

Cooking time: 10 minutes

Ingredients: 2 cups apple juice

1 cup stevia

2 tablespoons lemon zest, grated

2 pounds peaches, pitted and quartered

Directions: Heat up a pan over medium heat, add the apple juice and the rest of the ingredients, simmer for 10 minutes, transfer to a blender, pulse, divide into cups and keep in the freezer for 2 hours before serving.

Nutritional values per serving: Calories 182; Fat 5.4 g; Fiber 3.4 g; Carbs 12 g; Protein 5.4 g

Cranberries and Pears Pie

Servings: 4

Preparation time: 10 minutes

Cooking time: 40 minutes

Ingredients: 2 cup cranberries

3 cups pears, cubed

A drizzle of olive oil

1 cup stevia

1/3 cup almond flour

1 cup rolled oats

¼ avocado oil

Directions: In a bowl, mix the cranberries with the pears and the other ingredients except the olive oil and the oats, and stir well.

Grease a cake pan with the a drizzle of olive oil, pour the pears mix inside, sprinkle the oats all over and bake at 350° F for 40 minutes.

Cool the mix down, and serve.

Nutritional values per serving: Calories 172; Fat 3.4 g; Fiber 4.3 g; Carbs 11.5 g; Protein 4.5 g

Lemon Cream

Servings: 6

Preparation time: 1 hour

Cooking time: 10 minutes

Ingredients: 2 eggs, whisked

1 and ¼ cup stevia

10 tablespoons avocado oil

1 cup heavy cream

Juice of 2 lemons

Zest of 2 lemons, grated

Directions: In a pan, combine the cream with the lemon juice and the other ingredients, whisk well, cook for 10 minutes, divide into cups and keep in the fridge for 1 hour before serving.

Nutritional values per serving: Calories 200; Fat 8.5 g; Fiber 4.5 g; Carbs 8.6 g; Protein 4.5 g

Vanilla Cake

Servings: 10

Preparation time: 10 minutes

Cooking time: 25 minutes

Ingredients: 3 cups almond flour

3 teaspoons baking powder

1 cup olive oil

1 and ½ cup almond milk

1 and 2/3 cup stevia

2 cups water

1 tablespoon lime juice

2 teaspoons vanilla extract

Cooking spray

Directions: In a bowl, mix the almond flour with the baking powder, the oil and the rest of the ingredients except the cooking spray and whisk well.

Pour the mix into a cake pan greased with the cooking spray, introduce in the oven and bake at 370° F for 25 minutes. Leave the cake to cool down, cut and serve!

Nutritional values per serving: Calories 200; Fat 7.6 g; Fiber 2.5 g; Carbs 5.5 g; Protein 4.5 g

Pumpkin Cream

Servings: 2

Preparation time: 5 minutes

Cooking time: 5 minutes

Ingredients: 2 cups canned pumpkin flesh

2 tablespoons stevia

1 teaspoon vanilla extract

2 tablespoons water

A pinch of pumpkin spice

Directions: In a pan, combine the pumpkin flesh with the other ingredients, simmer for 5 minutes, divide into cups and serve cold.

Nutritional values per serving: Calories 192; Fat 3.4 g; Fiber 4.5 g; Carbs 7.6 g; Protein 3.5 g

Chia and Berries Smoothie Bowl

Servings: 2

Preparation time: 5 minutes

Cooking time: 0 minutes

Ingredients: 1 and ½ cup almond milk

1 cup blackberries

¼ cup strawberries, chopped

1 and ½ tablespoons chia seeds

1 teaspoon cinnamon powder

Directions: In a blender, combine the blackberries with the strawberries and the rest of the ingredients, pulse well, divide into small bowls and serve cold.

Nutritional values per serving: Calories 182; Fat 3.4 g; Fiber 3.4 g; Carbs 8 g; Protein 3 g

Minty Coconut Cream

Servings: 2

Preparation time: 4 minutes

Cooking time: 0 minutes

Ingredients: 1 banana, peeled

2 cups coconut flesh, shredded

3 tablespoons mint, chopped

1 and ½ cups coconut water

2 tablespoons stevia

½ avocado, pitted and peeled

Directions: In a blender, combine the coconut with the banana and the rest of the ingredients, pulse well, divide into cups and serve cold.

Nutritional values per serving: Calories 193; Fat 5.4 g; Fiber 3.4 g; Carbs 7.6 g; Protein 3 g

Watermelon Cream

Servings: 2

Preparation time: 15 minutes

Cooking time: 0 minutes

Ingredients: 1 pound watermelon, peeled and chopped

1 teaspoon vanilla extract

1 cup heavy cream

1 teaspoon lime juice

2 tablespoons stevia

Directions: In a blender, combine the watermelon with the cream and the rest of the ingredients, pulse well, divide into cups and keep in the fridge for 15 minutes before serving.

Nutritional values per serving: Calories 122; Fat 5.7 g; Fiber 3.2 g; Carbs 5.3 g; Protein 0.4 g

Grapes Stew

Servings: 4

Preparation time: 10 minutes

Cooking time: 10 minutes

Ingredients: 2/3 cup stevia

1 tablespoon olive oil

1/3 cup coconut water

1 teaspoon vanilla extract

1 teaspoon lemon zest, grated

2 cup red grapes, halved

Directions: Heat up a pan with the water over medium heat, add the oil, stevia and the rest of the ingredients, toss, simmer for 10 minutes, divide into cups and serve.

Nutritional values per serving: Calories 122; Fat 3.7; Fiber 1.2 g; Carbs 2.3 g; Protein 0.4 g

Cocoa Sweet Cherry Cream

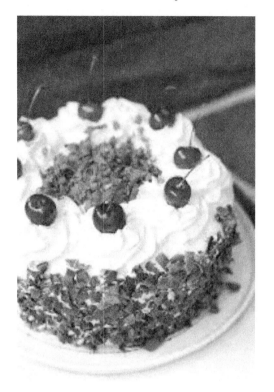

Servings: 4

Preparation time: 2 hours

Cooking time: 0 minutes

Ingredients: ½ cup cocoa powder

¾ cup red cherry jam

¼ cup stevia

2 cups water

1 pound cherries, pitted and halved

Directions: In a blender, mix the cherries with the water and the rest of the ingredients, pulse well, divide into cups and keep in the fridge for 2 hours before serving.

Nutritional values per serving: Calories 162; Fat 3.4 g; Fiber 2.4 g; Carbs 5 g; Protein 1 g

Apple Couscous Pudding

Servings: 4

Preparation time: 10 minutes

Cooking time: 25 minutes

Ingredients: ½ cup couscous

1 and ½ cups milk

¼ cup apple, cored and chopped

3 tablespoons stevia

½ teaspoon rose water

1 tablespoon orange zest, grated

Directions: Heat up a pan with the milk over medium heat, add the couscous and the rest of the ingredients, whisk, simmer for 25 minutes, divide into bowls and serve.

Nutritional values per serving: Calories 150; Fat 4.5 g; Fiber 5.5 g; Carbs 7.5 g; Protein 4 g

Ricotta Ramekins

Servings: 4

Preparation time: 10 minutes

Cooking time: 1 hour

Ingredients: 6 eggs, whisked

1 and ½ pounds ricotta cheese, soft

½ pound stevia

1 teaspoon vanilla extract

½ teaspoon baking powder

Cooking spray

Directions: In a bowl, mix the eggs with the ricotta and the other ingredients except the cooking spray and whisk well.

Grease 4 ramekins with the cooking spray, pour the ricotta cream in each and bake at 360° F for 1 hour.

Serve cold.

Nutritional values per serving: Calories 180; Fat 5.3 g; Fiber 5.4 g; Carbs 11.5 g; Protein 4 g

Papaya Cream

Servings: 2

Preparation time: 10 minutes

Cooking time: 0 minutes

Ingredients: 1 cup papaya, peeled and chopped

1 cup heavy cream

1 tablespoon stevia

½ teaspoon vanilla extract

Directions: In a blender, combine the cream with the papaya and the other ingredients, pulse well, divide into cups and serve cold.

Nutritional values per serving: Calories 182; Fat 3.1 g; Fiber 2.3 g; Carbs 3.5 g; Protein 2 g

Almonds and Oats Pudding

Servings: 4

Preparation time: 10 minutes

Cooking time: 15 minutes

Ingredients: 1 tablespoon lemon juice

Zest of 1 lime

1 and ½ cups almond milk

1 teaspoon almond extract

½ cup oats

2 tablespoons stevia

½ cup silver almonds, chopped

Directions: In a pan, combine the almond milk with the lime zest and the other ingredients, whisk, bring to a simmer and cook over medium heat for 15 minutes. Divide the mix into bowls and serve cold.

Nutritional values per serving: Calories 174; Fat 12.1 g; Fiber 3.2 g; Carbs 3.9 g; Protein 4.8 g

Chocolate Cups

Servings: 6

Preparation time: 2 hours

Cooking time: 0 minutes

Ingredients: ½ cup avocado oil

1 cup, chocolate, melted

1 teaspoon matcha powder

3 tablespoons stevia

Directions: In a bowl, mix the chocolate with the oil and the rest of the ingredients, whisk really well, divide into cups and keep in the freezer for 2 hours before serving.

Nutritional values per serving: Calories 174; Fat 9.1 g; Fiber 2.2 g; Carbs 3.9 g; Protein 2.8 g

Mango Bowls

Servings: 4

Preparation time: 30 minutes

Cooking time: 0 minutes

Ingredients: 3 cups mango, cut into medium chunks

½ cup coconut water

¼ cup stevia

1 teaspoon vanilla extract

Directions: In a blender, combine the mango with the rest of the ingredients, pulse well, divide into bowls and serve cold.

Nutritional values per serving: Calories 122; Fat 4 g; Fiber 5.3 g; Carbs 6.6 g; Protein 4.5 g

Cocoa and Pears Cream

Servings: 4

Preparation time: 10 minutes

Cooking time: 0 minutes

Ingredients: 2 cups heavy creamy

1/3 cup stevia

¾ cup cocoa powder

6 ounces dark chocolate, chopped

Zest of 1 lemon

2 pears, chopped

Directions: In a blender, combine the cream with the stevia and the rest of the ingredients, pulse well, divide into cups and serve cold.

Nutritional values per serving: Calories 172; Fat 5.6 g; Fiber 3.5 g; Carbs 7.6 g; Protein 4 g

Pineapple Pudding

Servings: 4

Preparation time: 10 minutes

Cooking time: 40 minutes

Ingredients: 3 cups almond flour

¼ cup olive oil

1 teaspoon vanilla extract

2 and ¼ cups stevia

3 eggs, whisked

1 and ¼ cup natural apple sauce

2 teaspoons baking powder

1 and ¼ cups almond milk

2 cups pineapple, chopped

Cooking spray

Directions: In a bowl, combine the almond flour with the oil and the rest of the ingredients except the cooking spray and stir well. Grease a cake pan with the cooking spray, pour the pudding mix inside, introduce in the oven and bake at 370° F for 40 minutes.

Serve the pudding cold.

Nutritional values per serving: Calories 223; Fat 8.1 g; Fiber 3.4 g; Carbs 7.6 g; Protein 3.4 g

Lime Vanilla Fudge

Servings: 6

Preparation time: 3 hours

Cooking time: 0 minutes

Ingredients:1/3 cup cashew butter

5 tablespoons lime juice

½ teaspoon lime zest, grated

1 tablespoons stevia

Directions: In a bowl, mix the cashew butter with the other ingredients and whisk well. Line a muffin tray with parchment paper, scoop 1 tablespoon of lime fudge mix in each of the muffin tins and keep in the freezer for 3 hours before serving.

Nutritional values per serving: Calories 200; Fat 4.5 g; Fiber 3.4 g; Carbs 13.5 g; Protein 5 g

Mixed Berries Stew

Servings: 6

Preparation time: 10 minutes

Cooking time: 15 minutes

Ingredients: Zest of 1 lemon, grated

Juice of 1 lemon

½ pint blueberries

1 pint strawberries, halved

2 cups water

2 tablespoons stevia

Directions: In a pan, combine the berries with the water, stevia and the other ingredients, bring to a simmer, cook over medium heat for 15 minutes, divide into bowls and serve cold.

Nutritional values per serving: Calories 172; Fat 7 g; Fiber 3.4 g; Carbs 8 g; Protein 2.3 g

Orange and Apricots Cake

Servings: 8

Preparation time: 10 minutes

Cooking time: 20 minutes

Ingredients: ¾ cup stevia

2 cups almond flour

¼ cup olive oil

½ cup almond milk

1 teaspoon baking powder

2 eggs

½ teaspoon vanilla extract

Juice and zest of 2 oranges

2 cups apricots, chopped

Directions: In a bowl, mix the stevia with the flour and the rest of the ingredients, whisk and pour into a cake pan lined with parchment paper.

Introduce in the oven at 375° F, bake for 20 minutes, cool down, slice and serve.

Nutritional values per serving: Calories 221; Fat 8.3 g; Fiber 3.4 g; Carbs 14.5 g; Protein 5 g

Blueberry Cake

Servings: 6

Preparation time: 10 minutes

Cooking time: 30 minutes

Ingredients: 2 cups almond flour

3 cups blueberries

1 cup walnuts, chopped

3 tablespoons stevia

1 teaspoon vanilla extract

2 eggs, whisked

2 tablespoons avocado oil

1 teaspoon baking powder

Cooking spray

Directions: In a bowl, combine the flour with the blueberries, walnuts and the other ingredients except the cooking spray, and stir well.

Grease a cake pan with the cooking spray, pour the cake mix inside, introduce everything in the oven at 350° F and bake for 30 minutes.

Cool the cake down, slice and serve.

Nutritional values per serving: Calories 225; Fat 9 g; Fiber 4.5 g; Carbs 10.2 g; Protein 4.5 g

Blueberry Yogurt Mousse

Servings: 4

Preparation time: 30 minutes

Cooking time: 0 minutes

Ingredients: 2 cups Greek yogurt

¼ cup stevia

¾ cup heavy cream

2 cups blueberries

Directions: In a blender, combine the yogurt with the other ingredients, pulse well, divide into cups and keep in the fridge for 30 minutes before serving.

Nutritional values per serving: Calories 141; Fat 4.7 g; Fiber 4.7 g; Carbs 8.3 g; Protein 0.8 g

Conclusion

Surely the Mediterranean diet is very effective thanks to the vegetables and whole-meal bread. If you have extra pounds, you will spontaneously eat less - especially if you take the time to chew well to activate your center of satiety - and you will lose them without a problem, without headache and frustration, above all. Also, you will be sure not to take them back because you will have integrated good eating habits. It's the right time to get started!

Printed in Great Britain
by Amazon